Antipoverty Effects of Unemployment Insurance

Thomas Gabe
Specialist in Social Policy

Julie M. Whittaker
Specialist in Income Security

October 4, 2012

Congressional Research Service

7-5700
www.crs.gov
R41777

Summary

This report examines the antipoverty effects of unemployment insurance benefits during the past recession and the economic recovery. The analysis highlights the impact of the additional and expanded unemployment insurance (UI) benefits available to unemployed workers through the American Recovery and Reinvestment Act (ARRA; P.L. 111-5) and the Emergency Unemployment Compensation (EUC08) program (Title IV of P.L. 110-252). In 2011, approximately 56% of all unemployed individuals were receiving UI benefits (down from a high of 66% in 2010) and thus were directly affected by legislative changes to the UI system. UI benefits appear to have a large poverty-reducing effect among unemployed workers who receive them. Given the extended length of unemployment among jobless workers, the additional weeks of UI benefits beyond the regular program's 26-week limit appear to have had an especially important effect in poverty reduction.

Estimates presented in this report are based on Congressional Research Service (CRS) analysis of 25 years of data from the U.S. Census Bureau's Annual Social and Economic Supplement to the Current Population Survey (CPS/ASEC), administered from 1988 to 2012. The period examined includes the three most recent economic recessions.

This report contributes to recent research on the antipoverty effects of unemployment insurance in several ways. Its period of analysis allows comparisons across the three most recent recessions. The report includes estimates of the effects on the poverty rate for the unemployed, for those receiving UI, and for families that report at least one family member receiving UI. It also estimates how much of reported UI benefits went directly to decreasing family poverty levels.

This report's analysis shows that UI benefits appear to reduce the prevalance of poverty significantly among the population that receives them. The UI benefits' poverty reduction effects appear to be especially important during and immediately after recessions. The analysis also finds that there was a markedly higher impact on poverty in the most recent recession than in the previous two recessionary periods. The estimated antipoverty effects of UI benefits in 2011 were about 50% higher than that of two previous peak years of unemployment—1993 and 2003.

- In 2011, over one quarter (26.5%) of unemployed people who received UI benefits would have been considered poor prior to taking UI benefits into account; after counting UI benefits, their poverty rate decreased by just under half, to 13.8%.

- UI receipt affects not only the poverty status of the person receiving the benefit, but the poverty status of all related family members, as well. In 2011, while an estimated 10.2 million people reported UI receipt during the year, an additional 15.8 million family members lived with the 10.2 million receiving the benefit. Consequently, UI receipt in 2011 affected the income status of some 26.0 million persons.

- In 2011, the poverty rate for persons in families who had received unemployment benefits was almost 40% less that it otherwise would have been.

In 2011, UI benefits lifted an estimated 2.3 million people out of poverty, of which well over one quarter (26.8%; 620,000) were children living with a family member who received UI benefits.

Contents

Figures

Tables

Appendixes

Contacts

Introduction

A period of unemployment greatly increases the odds that a worker and members of the worker's family will be counted among the nation's poor. For example, among persons between the ages of 16 and 64 who were unemployed in March 2012, about one in four (27.6%) were poor based on their families' incomes in 2011; among those who were employed, 6.9% were poor.[1]

A variety of social insurance benefits may be available for unemployed workers. The benefits analyzed in this report can be generically grouped into the category of Unemployment Insurance (UI) benefits. UI benefits provide a cash supplement to replace a portion of lost wages to qualified unemployed individuals. Two main objectives of the joint federal-state unemployment insurance program are to provide temporary and partial wage replacement to involuntarily unemployed workers and to stabilize the economy during recessions.[2]

As a temporary, partial replacement of lost earnings due to job loss, the benefits workers receive may help to prevent them and their family members from reaching poverty, an ancillary but important role of the program. Unemployment benefits are an individual worker's entitlement (as long as that worker meets the criteria for the benefit) and are not means tested.[3] In this regard, the UI program, while not a poverty program per se, can play an important role in reducing poverty associated with job loss.

In addition, as a countercyclical program UI has a macroeconomic effect in reducing poverty. By injecting dollars into the economy directed toward those who have experienced job loss, UI helps to partially mitigate income loss among a group directly affected by economic downturn. UI temporarily augments the ability of unemployed workers to meet basic needs, which further stimulates the economy. In this regard, the macroeconomic effect of UI helps dampen the tendency for poverty to increase during periods of economic downturn.

Roadmap

This report examines the antipoverty effects of UI benefits over the past three recessions. The analysis especially focuses on the most recent recession, from which the economy has only just begun to recover. It highlights the impact of the additional and expanded benefits available to unemployed workers in response to the most recent recession.

Estimates presented in this report are based on Congressional Research Service (CRS) analysis of 25 years of data from the U.S. Census Bureau's Annual Social and Economic Supplement to the Current Population Survey (CPS/ASEC), administered from 1988 to 2012. The period examined

---

[1] CRS Report RL33069, *Poverty in the United States: 2011*, by Thomas Gabe.

[2] See, for example, President Franklin Roosevelt's remarks at the signing of the Social Security Act at http://www.ssa.gov/?history/?fdrstmts.html#signing.

[3] By interpretation, entitlement to unemployment benefits cannot be restricted by means tests. See the Labor Secretary's interpretation on means testing and conformity to U.S. federal law http://ows.doleta.gov/dmstree/uipl/uipl_pre75/uipl_787.htm.

includes three economic recessions (July 1990 to March 1991, and March 2001 to November 2001, each lasting 8 months; and December 2007 to June 2009, lasting 18 months).[4]

In examining the role of UI benefits in alleviating poverty, this report does not consider any behavioral changes that individuals, employers, or government would have made had the UI benefit structure remained at permanent law levels throughout the period of analysis. In fact, if the temporary congressional changes in UI benefits had not existed, economic conditions would have been different. Some beneficiaries would have altered their behavior in a variety of ways. Some would have taken a job earlier or relied on additional hours of work from a spouse. Some would have chosen to terminate their job search earlier and move into retirement or apply for disability benefits. Absent the additional UI benefits, some might have qualified for other government benefits (e.g., food stamps) for which they otherwise would not have been eligible. In addition, some employers also would have made different decisions about hiring and laying off workers.

This report also ignores several important changes in the labor market that have affected both the unemployment rate and the poverty rate during this period. The aging of the labor market over time has generally decreased the unemployment rate. This decrease is tempered by the increased duration of unemployment as a result of the older profile of the labor market.[5] At the same time, workers are less likely to be laid off temporarily and more likely to become permanently separated from their former job.[6]

The report begins with a short section depicting labor market conditions over the 25-year period examined. The next section describes the Unemployment Insurance system, in terms of the permanent UI structure as well as the temporary measures Congress has enacted in reaction to poor economic conditions.

A third section examines the effect of UI benefit receipt on an individual's poverty status. It provides estimates of the number of persons who would fall below the nation's official income poverty threshold if UI benefits received were not counted as income. It also provides estimates on the number lifted above the poverty threshold and the share of unemployed persons who are poor, according to whether they received UI benefits during the year. A brief summary assesses the relative effects of the Unemployment Insurance system on poverty during the past recession compared with two preceding recessions.

The report contains three appendixes. **Appendix A** provides additional legislative details on the temporary measures enacted by Congress during the most recent recession—the Emergency Unemployment Compensation (EUC08) program.

---

[4] Periods of economic recession are officially designated by the National Bureau of Economic Research (NBER) Business Cycle Dating Committee. See http://www.nber.org/cycles/main.html.

[5] For an example, see U.S. Congress, House Committee on Ways and Means, Subcommittee on Income Security and Family Support, *What Does the Unemployment Rate Indicate About the Weak Labor Market?*, 110th Cong., 2nd sess., April 10, 2008, http://www.brookings.edu/~/media/Files/rc/testimonies/2008/0410_unemployment_blank/0410_unemployment_blank.pdf.

[6] For an example, see Chart 1 in Wayne Vroman, *The Great Recession, Unemployment Insurance and Poverty*, Urban Institute, Paper Prepared for the Conference on Reducing Poverty and Economic Distress after ARRA, Washington, DC, January 15, 2010, http://www.urban.org/uploadedpdf/412072_great_recession.pdf.

Appendix B provides data on trends in UI receipt by an individual's labor market status during a year. It provides contextual reference of different measures of labor "underutilization," including monthly and annual monthly averages of unemployment compared with estimates for persons unemployed at *any time during the year* (the definition of unemployed used in the report's CPS/ASEC analysis). It also examines more expansive definitions of labor utilization, which in addition to the unemployed (persons without a job who looked for work) includes involuntary part-time workers and discouraged workers (those who did not search for work, believing suitable work is not available). This appendix examines UI receipt reported on the CPS/ASEC among persons of the above, and other, labor force statuses.

Appendix C compares CPS/ASEC estimates to UI administrative data benchmarks. It assesses the relative quality of the CPS/ASEC UI estimates over the 25-year period examined in the report. The CPS/ASEC data undercount UI benefit receipt.[7] As a result, this report may underestimate the effect of unemployment insurance upon poverty rates.

Labor Market Context

Figure 1 depicts the U.S. monthly and annual average monthly unemployment rate[8] from January 1987 to August 2012. The figure shows that in each of the three recessions over the period, the unemployment rate is typically at a cyclical low just prior to the onset of economic recession, and it tends to continue to rise well beyond the recession's official end. As economic growth begins to take hold at a recession's end, employers are typically cautious in hiring new workers, waiting to be assured that economic growth is likely to persist. Job growth begins to take hold once existing labor capacity becomes stretched and the hiring of additional workers is required to meet increasing demand for employer-provided goods and services. The figure shows that in the 1990-1991 recession, unemployment rose from a pre-recession low of 5.0% in March 1989 to a post-recession high of 7.8% in June 1992, which was some 15 months after the recession's official end. In the subsequent 2000 recession, the unemployment rate rose from a pre-recession low of 3.8% in April 2000 to a high of 6.3% in June 2003, which was some 19 months after the recession's end. In the most recent recession, the unemployment rate rose from a pre-recession low of 4.4% in May 2007 to a post-recession high of 10.0% in October 2009, which was four months after the recession's official end. Almost three years since its most recent peak, the unemployment rate remained higher than the peak unemployment rate of the previous two recessions at 8.1% for August 2012.

---

[7] Bruce D. Meyer, Wallace K. C. Mok, and James X. Sullivan, *The Under-Reporting of Transfers in Household Surveys: Its Nature and Consequences*, National Bureau of Economic Research, NBER Working Paper no. 15181, July 2009, http://www.nber.org/papers/w15181.

[8] The unemployment rate measures the number of persons who are without a job or on layoff who are actively seeking work, as a percentage of the civilian labor force (the sum of employed and unemployed individuals). The monthly data have been seasonally adjusted.

Figure 1. Monthly and Annual Average Unemployment Rate
(January 1987 to August 2012)

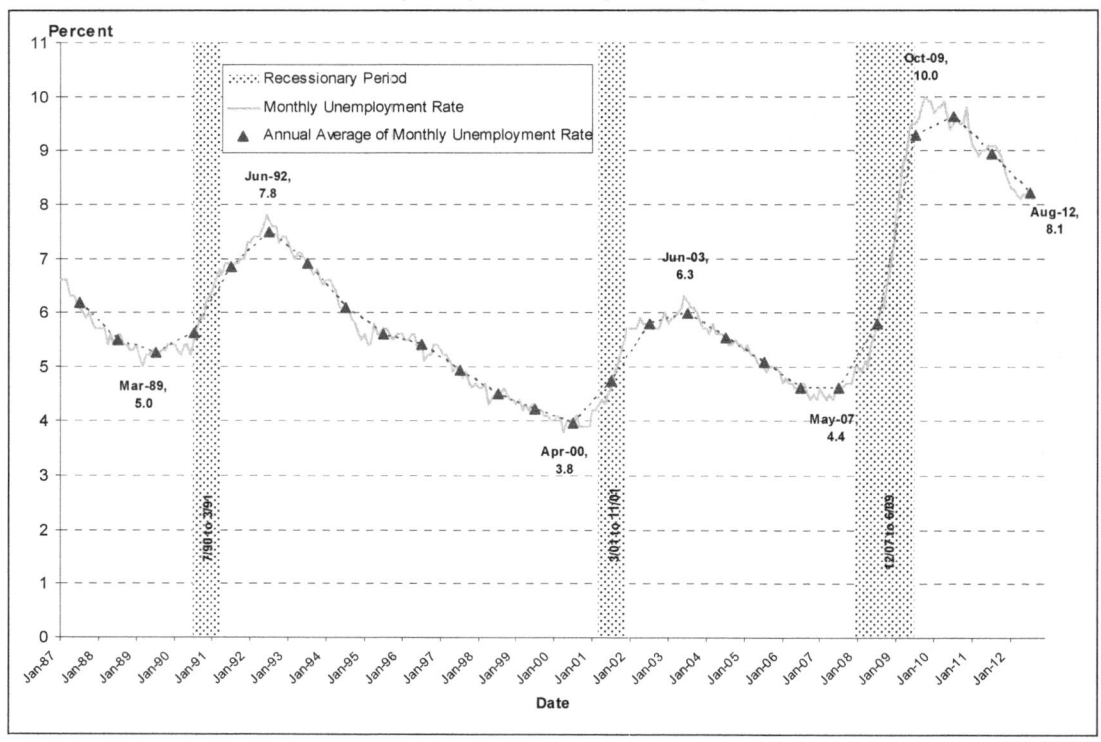

Source: Figure prepared by the Congressional Research Service (CRS) based on U.S. Bureau of Labor Statistics (BLS) monthly unemployment rates, available at http://data.bls.gov/cgi-bin/surveymost?bls. Monthly estimated unemployment rate has been seasonally adjusted.

In addition to the recession's length and sustained elevated unemployment rate, the duration of an individual's spell of unemployment is another indicator of labor market stress. **Figure 2** depicts the median number of weeks workers report having been unemployed. The figure shows that among unemployed workers, the peak median duration of unemployment for the most recent recession occurred in June 2010 and was 25.0 weeks. This suggests that at the peak over half of unemployed persons had been without work for just under six months. This peak was over twice as long as the two previous recessions (11.5 weeks in June 2003, and 10 weeks in October 1994).

Since peaking in June 2010, median duration of unemployment in August 2012 stood at 18.0 weeks.

Figure 2. Median Duration of Unemployment among Unemployed Workers in Weeks, January 1987 to August 2012

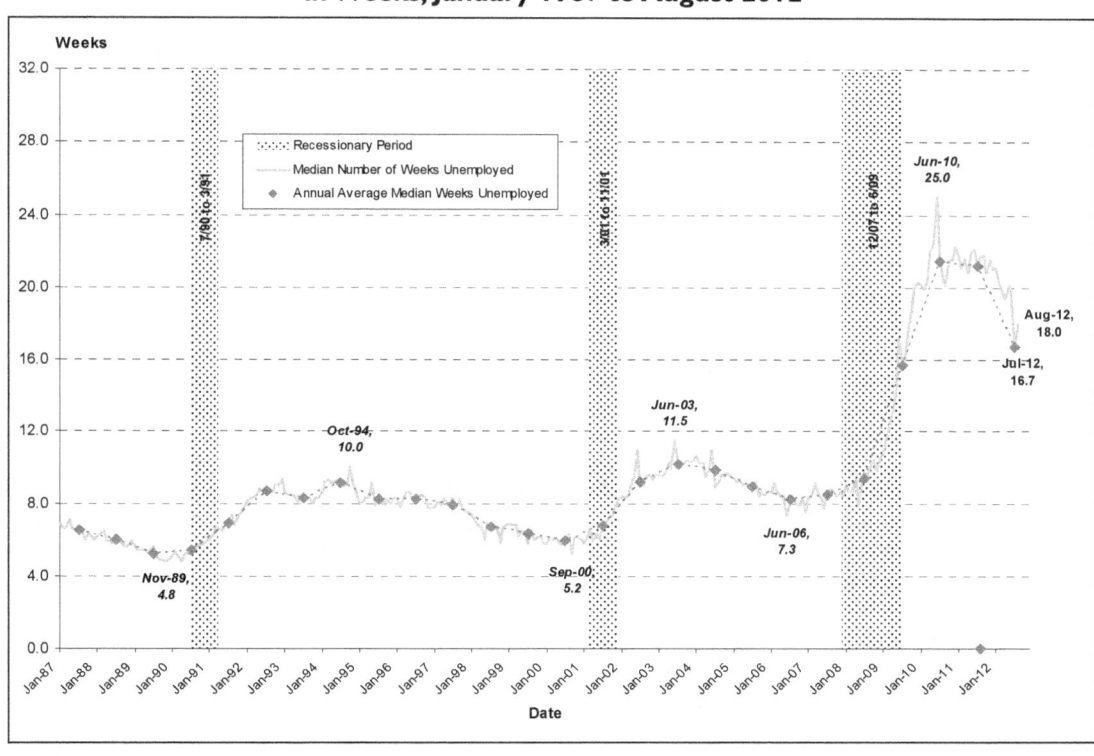

Source: Figure prepared by CRS based on BLS estimates.

An economic downturn may have other effects on the labor market than what is measured by the unemployment rate alone. For example, some former workers may drop out of the labor force all together and not bother to search for work, believing that no work is available and that job search would be fruitless—a category referred to as "discouraged workers." Others may have *recently searched* for work, but are *not currently looking* for work because of other impediments, such as transportation problems or problems with child care arrangements, that keep them from actively searching for a job. The Bureau of Labor Statistics (BLS) refers to this group as "marginally attached" workers. For some, an economic downturn may result in a situation where they are working part time but desire full-time work—a category sometimes referred to as "underemployed" or "employed part time for economic reasons."

In addition to the unemployment rate, the BLS publishes alternative measures of labor underutilization.[9] The most comprehensive alternative measure, U-6, includes the "unemployed" plus "discouraged" and other "marginally attached" workers, as well as persons who are "employed part time for economic reasons." The "official" unemployment rate is based on the total number of *unemployed* as a percentage of the *civilian labor force* (employed and unemployed workers, excluding the military). Under the alternative U-6 measure, "discouraged, marginally attached, and part-time workers for economic reasons" are added to the numerator of

---

[9] For a description of the alternative measures, see John E. Bregger and Steven E. Haugen, "BLS introduces new range of alternative unemployment measures," *Monthly Labor Review*, vol. 108, no. 10 (October 1995), pp. 19-26. Labor force statistics from the CPS, including alternative measures, are available at http://data.bls.gov/cgi-bin/surveymost?ln.

the "official" measure, and "discouraged and marginally attached" workers are added to the denominator.[10]

Figure 3 compares the BLS alternative U-6 rate of labor underutilization with the "official" unemployment rate. Estimates for the U-6 rate are first available in January 1994. In any period, the alternative expanded measure of labor underutilization, U-6, is considerably higher than the "official" unemployment rate; but in the wake of economic contractions, in particular, the U-6 measure emphasizes a heightened level of labor market distress compared with the unemployment rate alone. Over the period examined, the U-6 rate was, on average, 75% above the "official" unemployment rate, and it ranged from 63% (December 2002) to 83% (April 2008) above. In October 2009, for example, the unemployment rate was at an historical peak of 10.0%, while the U-6 labor underutilization rate, also at an historical peak, was 17.2%—7.2 percentage points (72%) above the "official" unemployment rate. In August 2012, the U-6 labor underutilization rate was 14.7%—5.6 percentage points (62%) above the "official" unemployment rate.

Figure 3. Seasonally Adjusted Unemployment Rate and an Alternative Measure of Underutilization (BLS U-6 Definition)

January 1987 to August 2012

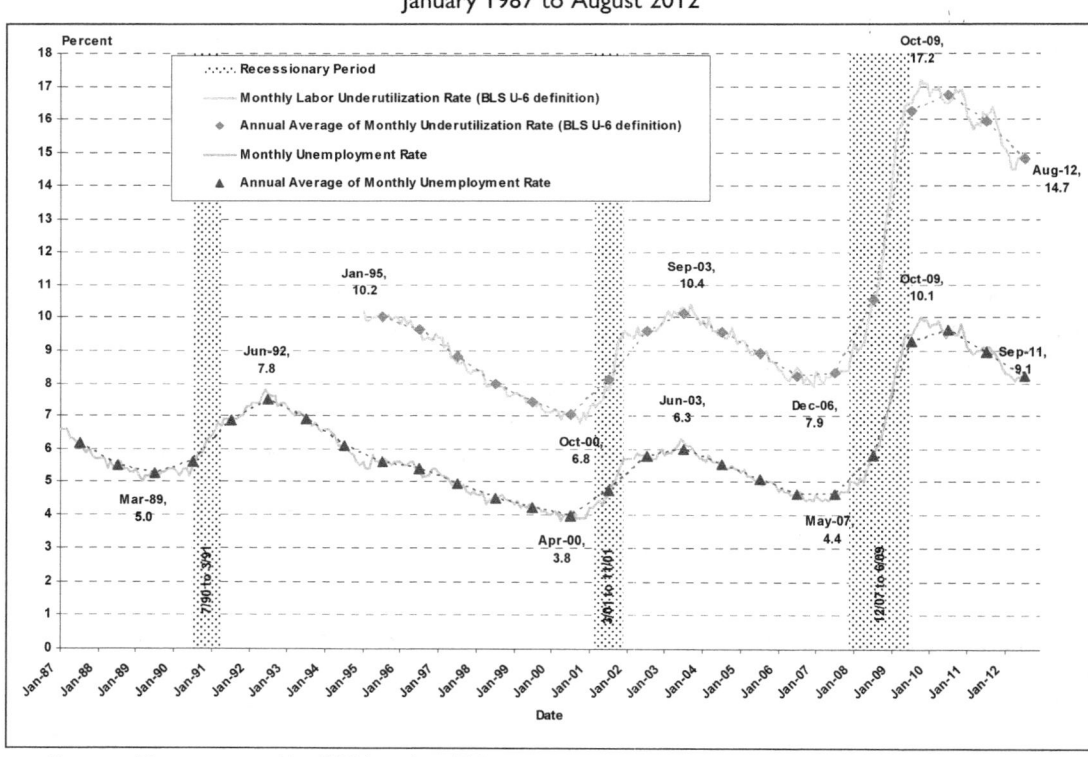

Source: Figure prepared by CRS based on BLS estimates.

Notes: The BLS alternative U-6 measure of labor underutilization includes unemployed, discouraged, marginally attached, and part-time workers desiring more work hours as a percent of an expanded labor force that includes all such persons in addition to employed workers.

---

[10] "Persons working part time for economic reasons" are already included in the civilian labor force definition used in the denominator of the "official" unemployment rate.

Unemployment Insurance

Workers who lose their jobs face serious long-term economic implications. In general, they face a substantially reduced probability of full-time employment and an increased probability of part-time employment. Permanently displaced workers (rather than job leavers or those who were on temporary lay-off) who find new full-time employment experience, on average, significantly decreased earnings relative to what they earned before they lost employment.[11]

A variety of benefits may be available for unemployed workers. Those examined in this report can be generically grouped into the category of Unemployment Insurance benefits,[12] which provide a cash supplement to replace a portion of lost wages to qualified unemployed individuals.[13] Most unemployed workers who receive benefits generally receive benefits from the Unemployment Compensation (UC) program first. Those who exhaust UC benefits may be eligible for additional weeks of unemployment insurance through the temporary Emergency Unemployment Compensation (EUC08) benefit or through the permanent extended benefit (EB) program.[14] These three benefits are often collectively referred to as Unemployment Insurance (UI) benefits. Generally, an unemployed worker would not notice a change in the type of benefit, as the weekly benefit amount remains constant while the funding stream or the legislative authority for the benefit changes as the unemployed worker moves from one benefit type to another over the course of his or her spell of unemployment.

Eligibility and Benefit Calculations for Unemployment Insurance Benefits

Federal laws and regulations provide broad guidelines on UC benefit coverage, eligibility, and benefit determination, but the specifics of regular UC benefits are determined by each state. This results in essentially 53 different programs.[15] States determine UC benefit eligibility, payments, and duration through state laws and program regulations. Generally, UC eligibility is based on

---

[11] For example see Lori G. Kletzer, "Job Displacement," *The Journal of Economic Perspectives*, vol. 12, no. 1 (Winter 1998), pp. 115-136 and Henry S. Farber, "What do we know about job loss in the United States? Evidence from the Displaced Workers Survey, 1984–2004," *Economic Perspectives: Federal Reserve Bank of Chicago*, vol. 29, no. 2 (2005), pp. 13-28.

[12] See CRS Report RL33362, *Unemployment Insurance: Programs and Benefits*, by Julie M. Whittaker and Katelin P. Isaacs for full details.

[13] For example, in addition to UI benefits, certain unemployed persons may qualify for continuation of group health insurance coverage under the Consolidated Omnibus Reconciliation Act of 1985 (COBRA; P.L. 99-272). See CRS Report: CRS Report R40142, *Health Insurance Continuation Coverage Under COBRA*, by Janet Kinzer. Also, certain workers who lose their jobs directly due to increased imports or shifts in production out of the United States may qualify for Trade Adjustment Assistance for Workers (TAA). See CRS Report R42012, *Trade Adjustment Assistance for Workers*, by Benjamin Collins.

[14] UC benefits may be extended at the state level by the permanent EB program if high unemployment exists within the state. Once regular unemployment benefits are exhausted, the EB program may provide up to an additional 13 or 20 weeks of benefits, depending on worker eligibility, state law, and economic conditions in the state. Under permanent law the EB program is funded 50% by the federal government and 50% by the states, although ARRA, as amended, temporarily provides for 100% federal funding of the EB program.

[15] The U.S. Department of Labor (DOL) administers the federal portion of the UC system, which operates in each state, the District of Columbia, Puerto Rico, and the Virgin Islands. Federal law sets broad rules that the 53 state programs must follow. These include the broad categories of workers that must be covered by the program, the method for triggering the EB and EUC08 programs, the floor on the highest state unemployment tax rate to be imposed on employers (5.4%), and how the states will repay Unemployment Trust Fund (UTF) loans.

attaining qualified wages and employment in covered work over a 12-month period (called a base period) prior to unemployment.

The UC program pays benefits to workers in covered employment who become involuntarily unemployed for economic reasons and meet state-established eligibility rules. The UC program generally does not provide UC benefits to the self-employed, to those who are unable to work, or to those who do not have a recent earnings history. States usually disqualify claimants who lost their jobs because of inability to work or unavailability for work, who voluntarily quit without good cause, who were discharged for job-related misconduct, or who refused suitable work without good cause.

This UC benefit is intended to help meet an unemployed worker's basic obligations until the worker finds a new position. Generally, states base benefit calculations on wages for covered work over a 12-month period, and in many states a full-time year-round worker would be eligible for 26 weeks of benefits.[16] The entitlement formula varies by state, typically requiring a substantial work history and replacing up to 50% of a worker's wages. Generally, benefits are capped at a percentage of the average wage for workers in the state and some states do not automatically link benefits to wage growth; these actions lowered the wage replacement rate for unemployment benefits to 33% of the average weekly wage in the second quarter of 2012.[17]

The permanent law EB program was established by the Federal-State Extended Unemployment Compensation Act of 1970 (EUCA; P.L. 91-373; 26 U.S.C. 3304, note). This program was intended to be the permanent law solution for automatically creating a federal response to economic downturns. The program may extend receipt of unemployment benefits (extended benefits) at the state level if certain economic situations exist within the state. Under permanent law, the costs of these benefits are shared—with 50% paid by federal funds and 50% by state funds.

All states must pay up to 13 weeks of EB if the insured unemployment rate[18] (IUR) for the previous 13 weeks is at least 5% and is 120% of the average of the rates for the same 13-week period in each of the two previous years. There are two other optional thresholds that states may choose. (States may choose one, two, or none.) If the state has chosen a given option, they would provide the following:

- Option 1: an additional 13 weeks of benefits if the state's IUR is at least 6%, regardless of previous years' averages.

---

[16] Several states provide fewer maximum weeks and two states (Massachusetts and Washington) provide additional weeks. For recent changes in benefit duration, see Table 1 in CRS Report R41859, *Unemployment Insurance: Consequences of Changes in State Unemployment Compensation Laws*, by Katelin P. Isaacs.

[17] See Employment and Training Administration, U.S. Department of Labor, *UI Data Summary*, 2nd Quarter 2012, Washington , DC, 2012. U.S. State Summary Table, http://ows.doleta.gov/unemploy/content/data_stats/datasum12/ DataSum_2012_2.pdf.

[18] The IUR is the ratio of UC claimants divided by individuals in UC-covered jobs. The IUR excludes several important groups: self-employed workers, unpaid family workers, workers in certain not-for-profit organizations, and several other, primarily seasonal, categories of workers. In addition to those unemployed workers whose last jobs were in the excluded employment, the insured unemployed rate excludes the following: those who have exhausted their UC benefits (even if they receive EB or EUC08 benefits); new entrants or reentrants to the labor force; disqualified workers whose unemployment is considered to have resulted from their own actions rather than from economic conditions; and, eligible unemployed persons who do not file for benefits.

- Option 2: an additional 13 weeks of benefits if the state's total unemployment rate[19] (TUR) is at least 6.5% and is at least 110% of the state's average TUR for the same 13 weeks in either of the previous two years; or an additional 20 weeks of benefits if the TUR is at least 8% and is at least 110% of the state's average TUR for the same 13 weeks in either of the previous two years.[20]

Recent studies have suggested that whether an IUR or TUR trigger is used, the secular decline in unemployment over the past several decades has resulted in the current trigger levels being relatively difficult to attain.[21] The current EB triggers have been criticized for deploying in many states long after a recession has started, for not deploying at all in some states with high unemployment, and for triggering off too quickly in some states. Analysts cite several reasons for this: (1) the general long-term decline in unemployment rates has made the current triggers irrelevant; (2) the rate and lookback provisions work against each other; and (3) amendments to the program in the early 1980s changed the unemployment calculation in a way that made EB activation less likely.[22]

Changes in the Structure and Generosity of Unemployment Insurance

This section briefly describes the various temporary unemployment benefit programs available in the last three recessions. Additionally, it attempts to explain how the current program and the ARRA provisions are intertwined and how they impact the amount of available unemployment benefits.

Temporary Federal Unemployment Insurance Programs, 1987-2012

In response to economic recessions, the federal government sometimes has augmented the regular (UC) benefit with both the permanent EB program and temporary expansions of unemployment benefits, including the current EUC08 program. These programs extended the duration (in addition to the potential maximum of up to 26 weeks of regular state UC benefits) an individual might claim benefits (up to an additional 20 weeks of EB and up to an additional 53 weeks of EUC08 throughout 2011, with several complicated changes in EUC08 during 2012). Some extensions took into account state economic conditions; many temporary programs considered the state's average unemployment rate or the state's insured unemployment rate, or both.[23]

---

[19] The TUR is the ratio of unemployed workers to all workers (employed and unemployed) in the labor market. The TUR is essentially a three-month averaged version of the unemployment rate published by the Bureau of Labor Statistics and based on data from the BLS' monthly Current Population Survey.

[20] P.L. 111-312, as amended made some temporary technical changes to certain triggers in the EB program, which allow states to temporarily use lookback calculations based on three years of unemployment rate data if states would otherwise trigger off or not be on a period of EB benefits. This temporary option to use three-year EB trigger lookbacks expires the week on or before December 31, 2012.

[21] See Jeffrey B. Wenger and Matthew J. Walters, "Why Triggers Fail (and What to Do About It): An Examination of the Unemployment Insurance Extended Benefits Program," *Journal of Policy Analysis and Management*, vol. 25, no. 3 (2006), pp. 553-575.

[22] The Omnibus Budget Reconciliation Act of 1981 redefined the IUR to remove UC exhaustees and EB beneficiaries from the numerator. The act also eliminated the national IUR trigger, and raised the states' trigger to 5%.

[23] CRS Report RL34340, *Extending Unemployment Compensation Benefits During Recessions*, by Julie M. Whittaker and Katelin P. Isaacs.

From 1987 through 2012, there were three temporary programs that were in effect at different times. **Table 1** on the following page provides basic information on the programs' beginning and ending dates, and the lowest maximum duration and highest maximum duration for potential receipt of benefits during the programs' existences. The 1991 Emergency Unemployment Compensation (EUC) program provided a maximum of between 13 and 33 weeks of benefits over its duration. The 2002 Temporary Emergency Unemployment Compensation (TEUC) program provided up to 26 weeks of temporary benefits for its duration. The current EUC08 program began in July 2008 and provided up to 20 weeks of benefits; over time the program has been modified several times to provide up to 53 weeks of benefits (63 weeks for a few months in 2012, 47 weeks as of September 2012). Additionally, ARRA supplemented all unemployment benefits with an additional $25/week benefit (Federal Additional Compensation [FAC]) from March 2009 through May 2010.

Table 1. General Description of Temporary Federal Unemployment Insurance Programs, 1987- 2012

	1990-1991 Recession	2001 Recession	2007 Recession
	P.L. 102-164, EUC Benefits	**P.L. 107-147, TEUC Benefits**	**P.L. 110-252, EUC08 Benefits**
Congress first enacts extension	August 1991	February 2002	June 2008
Program becomes active	November 1991[a,b]	March 2002	July 2008
Minimum weeks of benefits available	13 Weeks	26 Weeks	13 Weeks
	December 1993-February 1994	November 2001-January 2004	July 2008-November 2008
Maximum weeks of benefits available	33 Weeks	26 Weeks	53 Weeks
	November 1991-July 1992	November 2001-January 2004	Beginning December 2009-February 2012 and June-August 2012
			(63 weeks, February 2012-May 2012; 47 weeks beginning in September 2012)
Authorization ended (does not include phase out)	February 1994	January 2004	Scheduled: End of December 2012

Source: Congressional Research Service (CRS). Timing of recessions from National Bureau of Economic Research, http://www.nber.org/cycles.html.

a. H.R. 3201 was passed on August 2, 1991; President George H.W Bush signed the bill (P.L. 102-107) but did not declare an emergency; thus, no benefits were available. Congress sent S. 1722 to the President who vetoed it on October 1, 1991. For a statement on the reasons for the veto, see http://www.presidency.ucsb.edu/ws/index.php?pid=20097.

b. Although P.L. 102-164 was signed into law on November 15, 1991, it was immediately superseded by two other laws: P.L. 102-182, signed December 4, 1991, and P.L. 102-244, signed February 7,1992. P.L. 102-182 authorized benefit periods of 20 and 13 weeks depending on state economic conditions; P.L. 102-244 authorized an additional 13 weeks for each tier.

Interaction of the American Recovery and Reinvestment Act of 2009 (ARRA; P.L. 111-5) with Unemployment Insurance

ARRA contained several provisions affecting unemployment benefits. Through the FAC program, ARRA temporarily increased all types of unemployment benefits, by $25 per week for all recipients of any type of unemployment insurance,[24] and excluded $2,400 in UI benefits from gross income under the federal income tax for 2009. ARRA extended the temporary EUC08 program through December 26, 2009 (with grandfathering). The EUC08 program's expiration date has since been extended further, through December 29, 2012.

ARRA, as amended, provides for temporary 100% federal financing of the permanently authorized EB program through December 31, 2012. It also allows states the option of temporarily ignoring the programmatic "benefit year" requirement.[25] Instead, states can choose to use exhaustion of EUC08 benefits as an eligibility requirement for weeks of EB benefit payments that fall between ARRA's enactment and expiration of 100% federal funding of the EB program, and as long as the state was triggered "on" for EB during the period when the individual was receiving EUC08.[26] This has the effect of allowing more individuals to be eligible for the EB program.[27] States have been able to take advantage of this temporary financing structure by linking optional ways to have an active EB program with the temporary ARRA 100% federal financing scheme for EB.[28] Furthermore, ARRA prohibited states from decreasing average weekly benefits.[29]

In addition, ARRA provided up to a total of $7 billion in "modernization" payments as incentives to states to modify their basis for computing UI benefits and for extending benefits to currently ineligible individuals. Two-thirds of the $7 billion available to states was contingent on states first adopting an alternative method of determining eligibility for individuals who do not qualify under the regular method based on their wage and employment history.[30] The states were then eligible for the remaining two-thirds of the $7 billion if they adopted at least two of the following four provisions:

---

[24] Regular state unemployment benefits averaged just over $300 during the period the FAC was offered. An additional $25 would be approximately an 8% increase for an average benefit. Regardless of the state determined weekly benefit amount, each worker receiving any type of unemployment benefit would have received an additional $25 each week.

[25] Under permanent law, the benefit year is a one-year period during which a worker may receive benefits based on a previous period of unemployment. In all states, the beginning date of the benefit year depends on when a worker first files a valid claim, meaning the worker met state determined minimal earnings and employment requirements.

[26] Under permanent law the EB program is "triggered on" when a state's unemployment level reaches certain levels. All states must pay up to 13 weeks of EB if the insured unemployment rate (a programmatic measure) for the previous 13 weeks is at least 5% and is 120% of the average of the rates for the same 13-week period in each of the two previous years. There are two other optional thresholds that states may choose. Additionally, P.L. 111-312, as amended, allows states to opt for a three-year lookback calculation. This option expires on December 31, 2012.

[27] All states opted for this calculation.

[28] A total of 28 states opted for a temporary trigger. As of September 27, 2012, only New York state had an active EB program.

[29] When the FAC benefit was not extended by the amendments to ARRA in P.L. 111-205, the "non-reduction" rule for weekly benefits was placed as an amendment to EUC08 (P.L. 110-252).

[30] Information on state applications to receive the modernization payments and a summary of state actions to expand potential entitlement to unemployment benefits can be found under the "UI Modernization Incentive Payments" on the webpage: http://ows.doleta.gov/unemploy/laws.asp.

---

1. permit former part-time workers to seek part-time work;

2. permit voluntary separations from employment for compelling family reasons, which must include (1) domestic violence, (2) illness or disability of an immediate family member, and (3) the need to accompany a spouse who is relocating for employment;

3. provide extended compensation to UC recipients in qualifying training programs for high-demand occupations; or

4. provide dependents' allowances to UC recipients with dependents.

A total of 36 states received the full amount available to them under the modernization law. An additional 5 states received the first one-third payment for allowing an alternative base period calculation. A total of $4.4 billion was distributed to these 41 states.[31]

How Important Were the Temporary Programs to the Unemployed?

It is difficult to assess the exact monetary impact of ARRA and the EUC08 program on the unemployed. However, data do exist to explain what percentage of the unemployed received unemployment benefits that were deployed on account of high unemployment (either the temporary benefit or the EB benefit). **Figure 4** displays two data series. The lower line is the percentage of unemployed persons who received the regular (up to the first 26 weeks) state UC benefit. The upper line includes this group combined with the unemployed who received additional temporary unemployment benefits (such as the EUC08 benefit) and the EB payments.

Generally, as a recession winds down the percentage of unemployed who are receiving regular UC declines, as most of the unemployed are the long-term unemployed who have exhausted benefits or are new (or returning) labor market participants who may be ineligible for regular UC benefits. The percentage of the unemployed receiving *any* UI benefit continues to increase as the proportion of long-term unemployed in the pool of unemployed workers increases. The ARRA provisions and the EUC08 program temporarily expanded both the potential amount and the duration of unemployment benefits, exceeding the generosity of any previous congressional intervention. This can be seen in the increased percentage of the unemployed receiving UI benefits in 2009 and 2010—almost two-thirds of all unemployed persons were receiving unemployment benefits (the highest level since 1976). The percentage of unemployed workers receiving unemployment benefits declined in 2011, continued to be above half (56%) of all unemployed workers.

---

[31] See http://ows.doleta.gov/unemploy/laws.asp#modern for exact sums distributed to the 41 states.

Figure 4. Percentage of Unemployed Receiving Unemployment Benefits
1987-2012

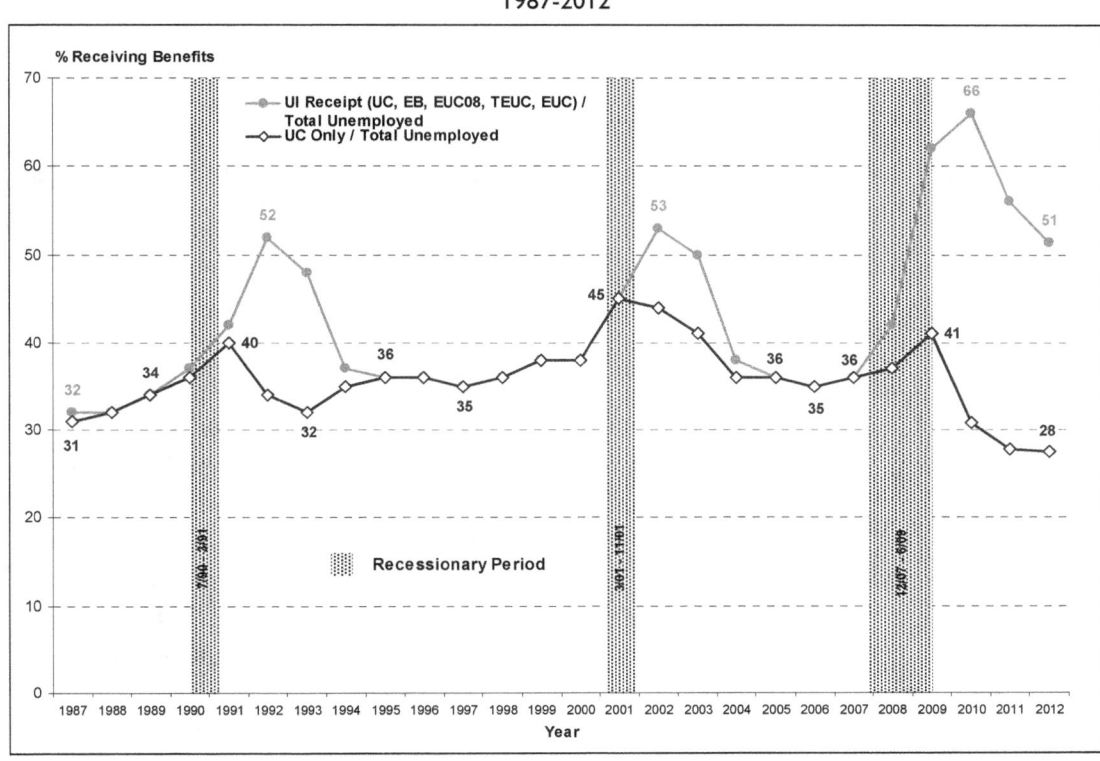

Source: Figure created by CRS from U.S. Department of Labor data.

Note: 2012 data are for January 2012-July 2012.

Figure 5 depicts the average percentage of workers who received some kind of additional benefit beyond regular UC payments. In 2010, the percentage of unemployed who received additional benefits beyond regular UC (35%) was at least 17 percentage points higher than any other year in the previous two post-recession periods. By 2012, the percentage had dropped to 24%, which was still 6 percentage points higher than any other year in the previous two post-recession periods.

Figure 5. Percentage of Unemployed Receiving Temporary (EUC, TEUC, or EUC08) Benefits or Extended Benefits

1987-2012

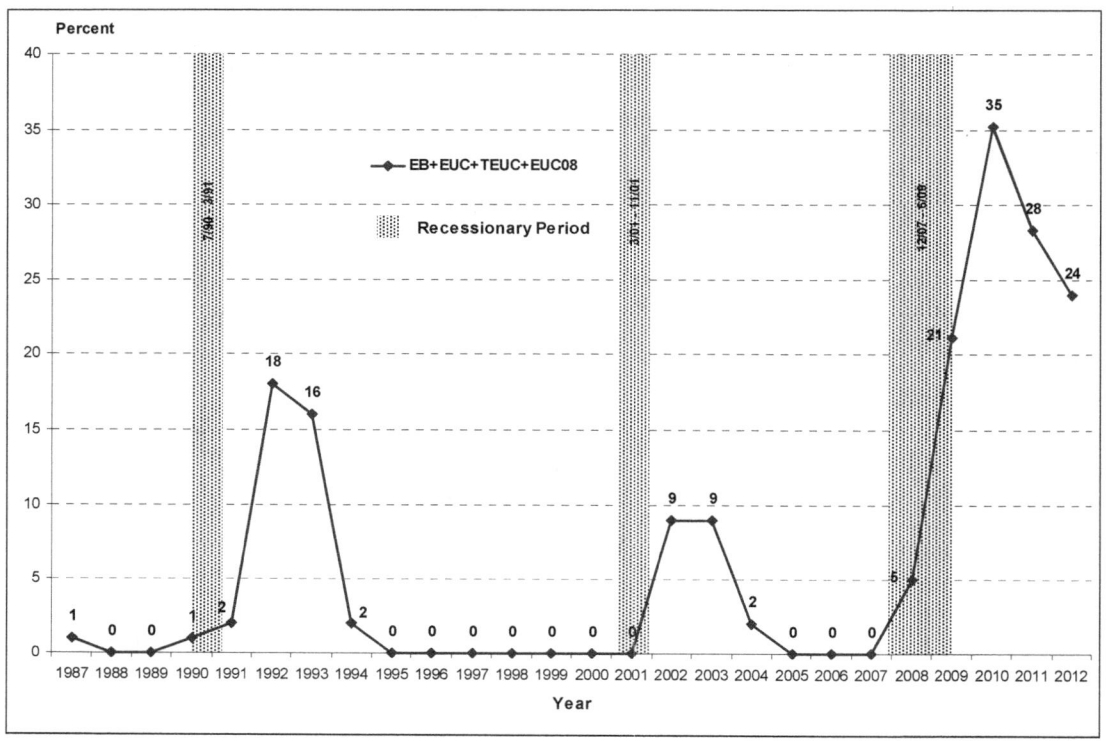

Source: Figure created by CRS from U.S. Department of Labor data.

Note: 2012 data are for January 2012-July 2012.

Antipoverty Effects of Unemployment Insurance

The role unemployment insurance plays in poverty among the unemployed is well documented. A Congressional Budget Office (CBO) study found that the UI benefits reduced the 2009 poverty rate by 1.1 percentage points to 14.3%.[32] Recent research by Vroman examined UI benefits and all other types of federal transfer payments from 2001 through 2008 and found that while the overall effect on the poverty rate was small the impact increases as the duration of unemployment

---

[32] Gregory Acs and Molly Dahl, *Unemployment Insurance Benefits and Family Income of the Unemployed*, Congressional Budget Office, Washington, DC, November 17, 2010, http://www.cbo.gov/ftpdocs/119xx/doc11960/11-17-UnemploymentInsurance.pdf.

increases.[33] In a brief analysis of the impact of the 2009 American Recovery and Reinvestment Act (P.L. 111-5), Sherman estimated that 1.3 million people were kept out of poverty through additional temporary UI benefits.[34]

This report contributes to this recent research on the antipoverty effects of unemployment insurance in several ways. Its period of analysis is longer and allows comparisons across the three most recent recessions. The report includes estimates of the effects on the poverty rate for the unemployed, those receiving UI, and for families that report at least one family member receiving UI. It also estimates how much of the total reported UI benefits went directly to decreasing family poverty levels.

Antipoverty Effects of UI on All Related Persons

This section examines the antipoverty effects of UI benefits primarily for all persons who received UI benefits (not just those who had limited labor force attachment due to economic reasons). Because the U.S. poverty measure is based on the income of all co-resident related family members, UI receipt affects not only the poverty status of the person receiving the benefit, but the poverty status of all related family members, as well. In 2011, while an estimated 10.2 million people reported UI receipt during the year,[35] an additional 15.8 million family members lived with the 10.2 million receiving the benefit. Consequently, UI receipt in 2011 affected the income status of some 26.0 million persons.

Figure 6 shows the effect of UI benefit receipt on the overall poverty rate. The figure shows the percentage of persons in poverty—both before counting UI benefits as income and after—using Census Bureau poverty income thresholds.[36] The figure shows, for example, that in 2011, under the pre-UI benefit poverty measure, an estimated 15.7% of the population would have been counted as poor; the receipt of UI benefits reduced the poverty rate by 0.7 percentage points, to 15.0%, the "official" U.S. poverty rate. The antipoverty effect of UI benefits was somewhat reduced in 2011 as compared with 2010 (a 1.1 percentage point reduction, from 16.2% to 15.1%), reflecting the general trend of decreasing percentages of the unemployed receiving UI benefits. Note that 1993 marked a previous peak in the "official" poverty rate, at 15.1%, but UI benefits contributed to only a 0.5 percentage point reduction in poverty (i.e., from 15.6% to 15.1%) in that year. By this measure, the poverty reducing effect of UI in both 2009 and 2010 was about twice that of 1993, although by 2011 the effect was substantially muted.

---

[33] Wayne Vroman, *The Great Recession, Unemployment Insurance and Poverty*, Urban Institute, Paper Prepared for the Conference on Reducing Poverty and Economic Distress after ARRA, Washington, DC, January 15, 2010, http://www.urban.org/uploadedpdf/412072_great_recession.pdf.

[34] Arloc Sherman, Despite Deep Recession and High Unemployment, Government Efforts, -Including the Recovery Act- Prevented Poverty from Rising in 2009, New Census Data Show, Center on Budget and Policy Priorities, Washington, DC, January 5, 2011, http://www.cbpp.org/cms/index.cfm?fa=view&id=3361.

[35] An estimated 8.1 million (79.4%) of those persons had limited or no attachment to a job during the year, due to economic reasons; i.e., were unemployed, worked fewer hours than desired, or were "discouraged" potential workers. (See **Appendix B** for more information UI benefit receipt by labor force status on the CPS/ASEC.)

[36] Census Bureau poverty thresholds vary by family size and composition. In 2011, for example, the average poverty threshold for single persons living with no related family members was $11,484; for two related persons, $14,657, for three related persons, $17,916 and for four related persons, $23,021.

Figure 6. Pre- and Post-UI Benefit Poverty Rates of Persons, 1987-2011

Percentage of persons who are poor before and after counting UI benefits

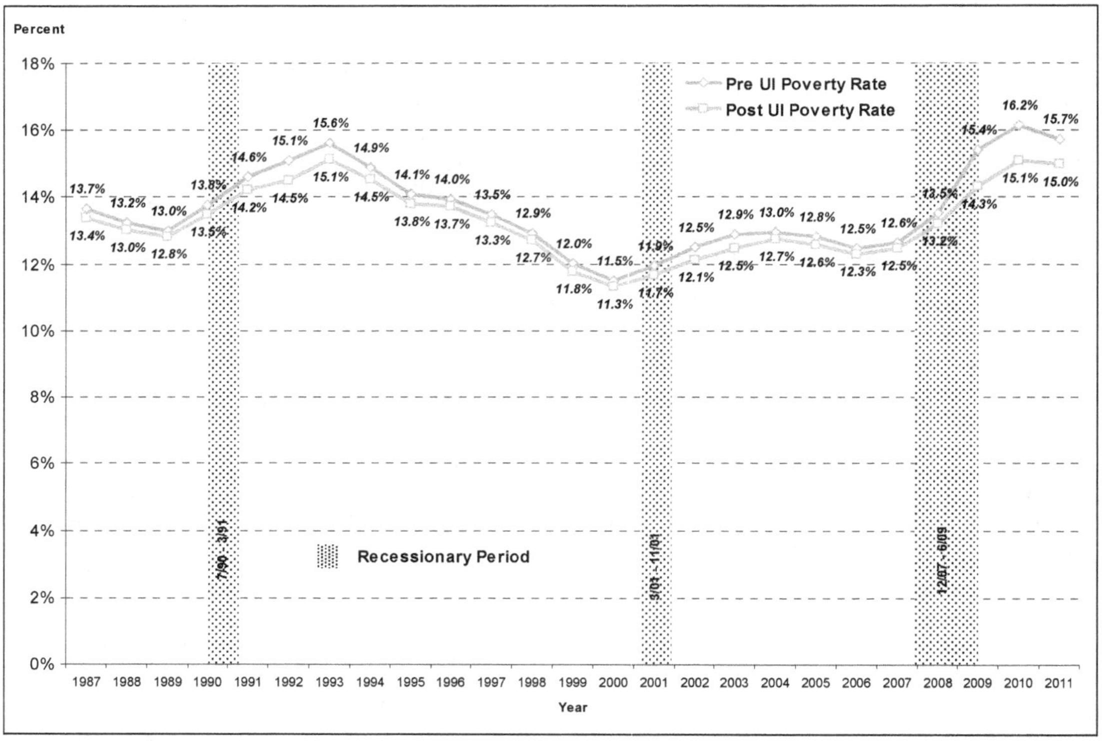

Source: CRS estimates from U.S. Census Bureau Current Population Survey Annual Social and Economic Supplement (CPS/ASEC), 1988 to 2012.

Figure 7 shows the number of persons (in millions) lifted above poverty by the receipt of UI benefits. The figure shows that in both 2009 and 2010, well over 3 million people (3.3 and 3.2 million, respectively) were lifted above the official poverty line as the result of UI benefit receipt. The number of persons lifted above the official poverty line in 2011 was lower than in the previous two years; but it was still substantial at just over 2.3 million. UI benefits lifted nearly a million children (956,000) above the poverty line in 2009. In 2010 and 2011, the number of children lifted about the poverty line declined to 861,000 and 620,000, respectively. In contrast, in 1992, UI lifted about 1.5 million persons out of poverty, of whom nearly a half million (479,000) were children.

Figure 7. Number of Persons Lifted Above Poverty as a Result of UI Benefit Receipt, 1987-2011

millions of persons

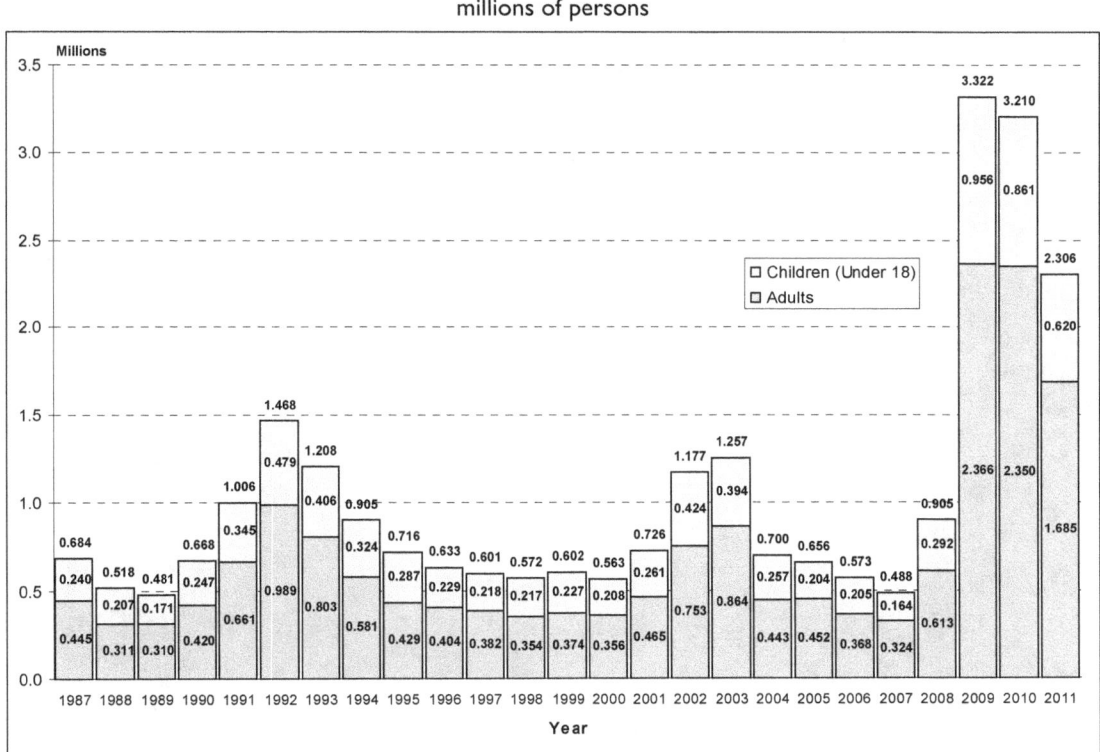

Source: CRS estimates from CPS/ASEC, 1988 to 2012.

Antipoverty Effect of UI on Persons in Families Receiving UI Benefits

Figure 8 shows pre- and post-UI poverty rates among persons in which they or another family member received UI benefits during the year. The figure is similar to **Figure 6**, except that figure showed the effect of UI benefit receipt on the overall U.S. poverty rate, whereas **Figure 8** is only for persons in families that received UI benefits. The figure shows, for example, that in 2011, among individuals and families in which someone received UI benefits during the year, well over one-fifth of persons (22.5%) would have been considered poor absent the UI benefits they received; UI benefits cut their prevalence of poverty by almost 9 percentage points to between one in seven and one in eight persons (13.6%).

Figure 8. Pre- and Post-UI Benefit Poverty Rates of Persons in Families that Received UI Benefits, 1987-2011

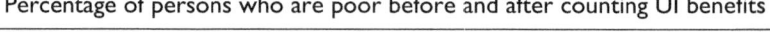

Percentage of persons who are poor before and after counting UI benefits

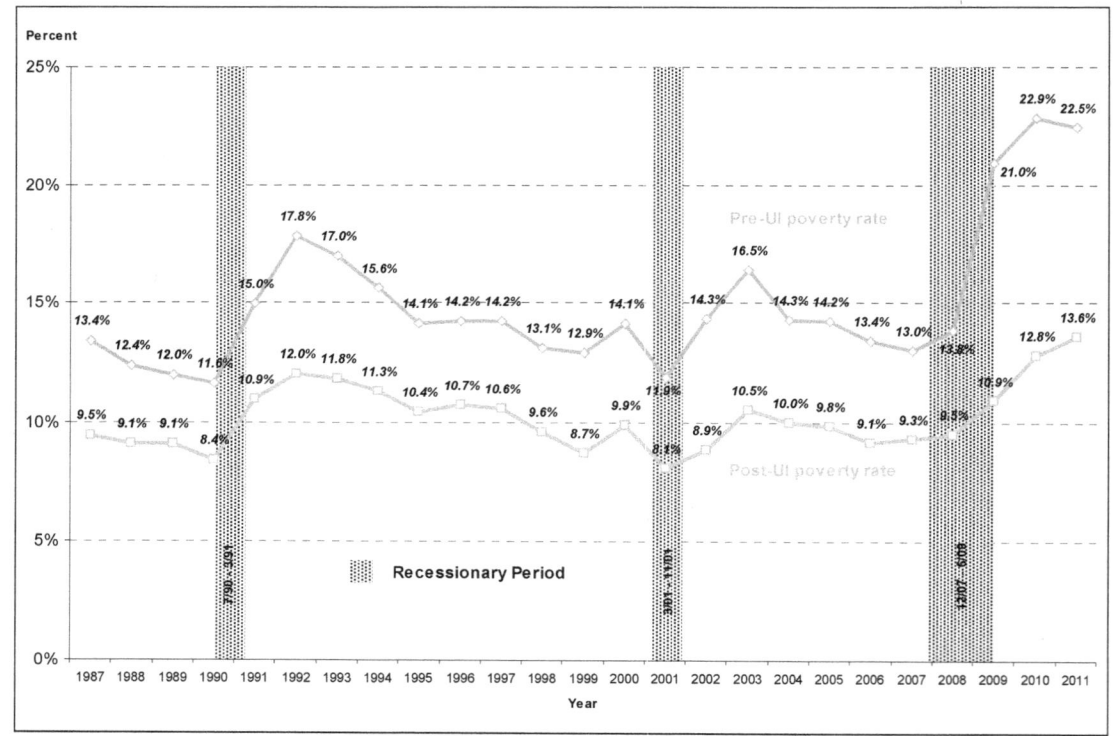

Source: CRS estimates from U.S. Census Bureau Current Population Survey Annual Social and Economic Supplement (ASEC), 1988 to 2012.

Figure 9 shows calculations derived from the data presented in **Figure 6** and **Figure 8**. **Figure 9** shows that UI benefits in 2009, 2010, and 2011 reduced the overall poverty rate by 7.1% ,6.5%, and 4.7%, respectively—in 2009, almost twice the next largest reduction of poverty attributable to UI benefits in 1992, when UI cut the overall poverty rate by 3.8%. Among persons in families and unrelated individuals that received UI benefits, those benefits cut their poverty rate nearly in half (48.0%) in 2009, by 44.0% in 2010, and by 39.4% in 2011, compared with about two-fifths (38.1%) in 2002, and about one-third in 1992 (32.5%).

Figure 9. Percentage Reduction in the Poverty Rate as a Result of UI Benefit Receipt, Overall Poverty Rate and Poverty Rate for Persons in Families that Received UI Benefits, 1987 - 2011

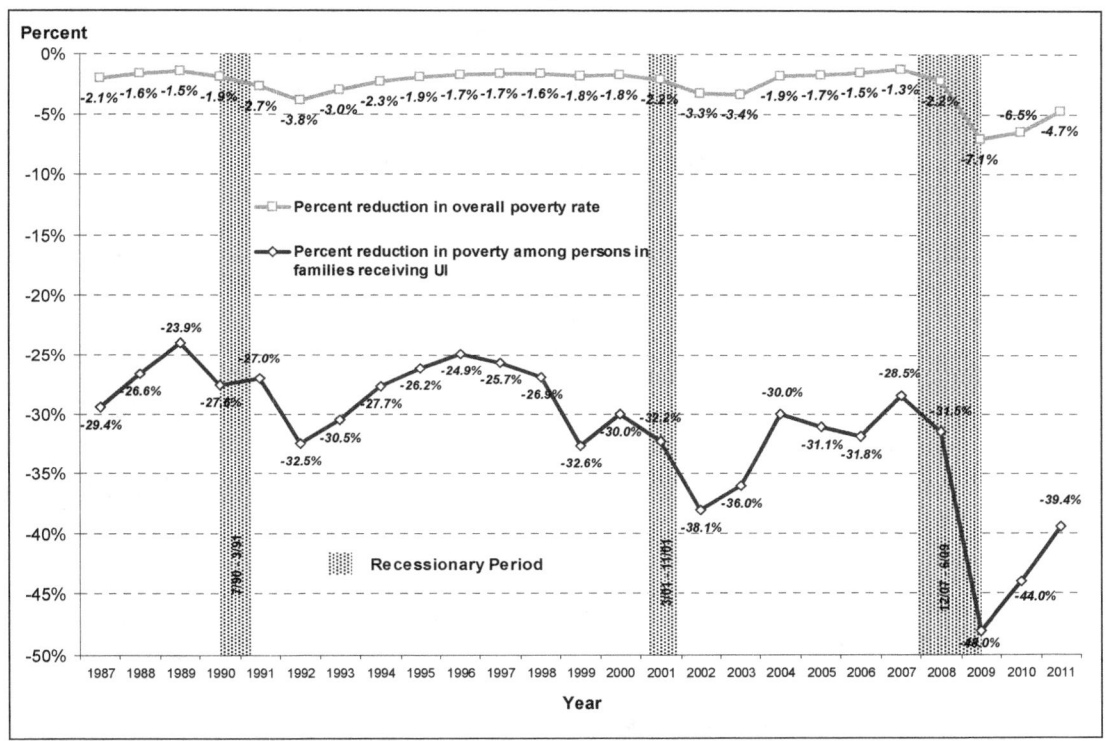

Source: CRS estimates from CPS/ASEC, 1988 to 2012.

Aggregate UI Dollars Going Toward Reducing Poverty

Figure 10 shows that aggregate UI benefits reported on the CPS in 2009 and 2010 ($102.3 billion and $98.5 billion, respectively in 2011 constant dollars) were over twice those reported in 1992 ($43.8 billion in 2011 constant dollars) and in 2002 ($46.6 billion in 2011 constant dollars). Aggregate UI benefits in 2011 ($68.5 billion) decreased from the previous two years but were still substantially above previous recession's peaks. In 2009, an estimated $18.5 billion in UI benefits went towards reducing poverty[37] (18.1% of all UI dollars), $20.0 billion in 2010 (20.3% of all UI dollars), and $14.8 billion in 2011 (21.6% of all UI dollars). In 1992, about $7.3 billion (16.7% of all UI dollars), and in 2003, an estimated $6.0 billion (13.6% of all UI dollars) went toward poverty reduction. Notice that actual benefits paid out exceed the amount captured by the CPS/ASEC, as income amounts from virtually all income sources reported on the survey tend to fall short of administrative or other benchmarks (see **Appendix C** for further discussion).

Figure 10. UI Benefits: Aggregate Dollars and Dollars Reducing Poverty, 1987-2011

(in billions of 2011 constant dollars)

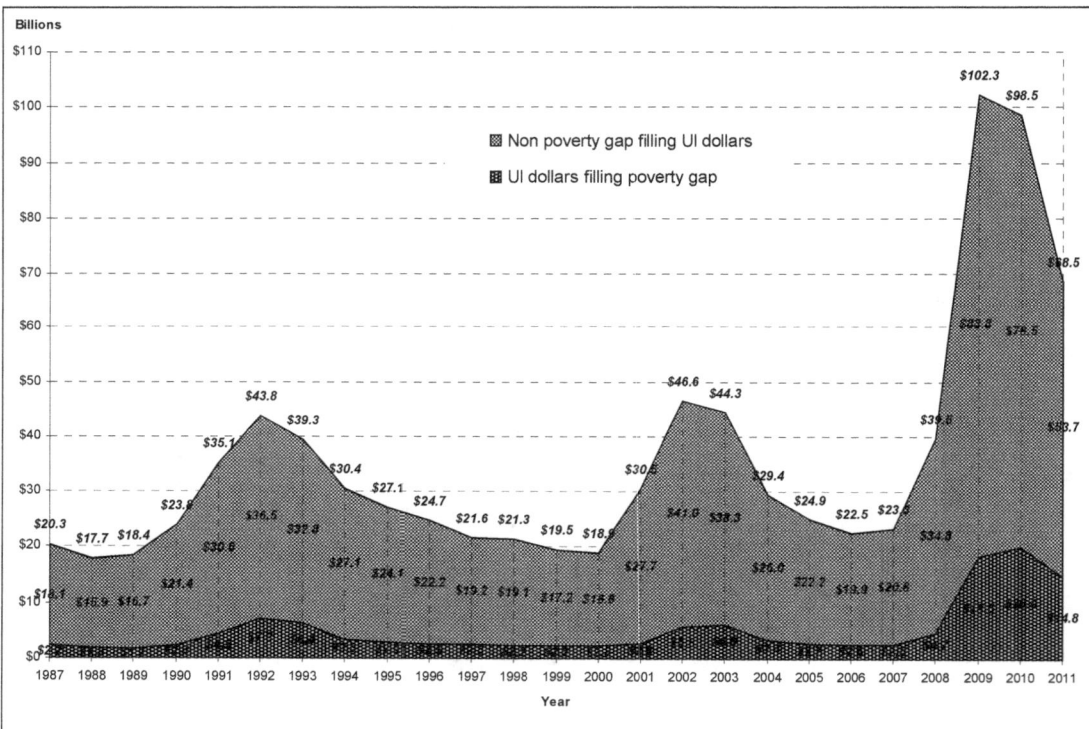

Source: CRS estimates from CPS/ASEC, 1988 to 2012.

Note: Dollars are estimates reported on the CPS/ASEC, which under-represent actual benefits paid to the unemployed. Among families considered poor before counting any UI benefits they received UI dollars filling the "poverty gap" represent the aggregate amount of UI benefits going towards filling the shortfall in families' incomes from their respective poverty income thresholds.

---

[37] Among families considered poor before counting any UI benefits they received, UI dollars filling the "poverty gap" represent the aggregate amount of UI benefits going towards filling the shortfall in families' incomes from their respective poverty income thresholds.

Figure 11 uses calculations from the data presented in **Figure 10** to show the proportion of UI dollars that reduced poverty to all UI dollars. **Figure 11** shows, for example, that even though aggregate UI benefits received by families decreased from 2011 to 2010 (**Figure 10**) the share that went towards poverty reduction increased to an historic peak (21.6%) in 2011. In 2011, over one-fifth of UI benefits families' received went toward reducing poverty.

Figure 11. Share of Aggregate UI Benefits Going Toward Reducing Poverty, 1987-2011

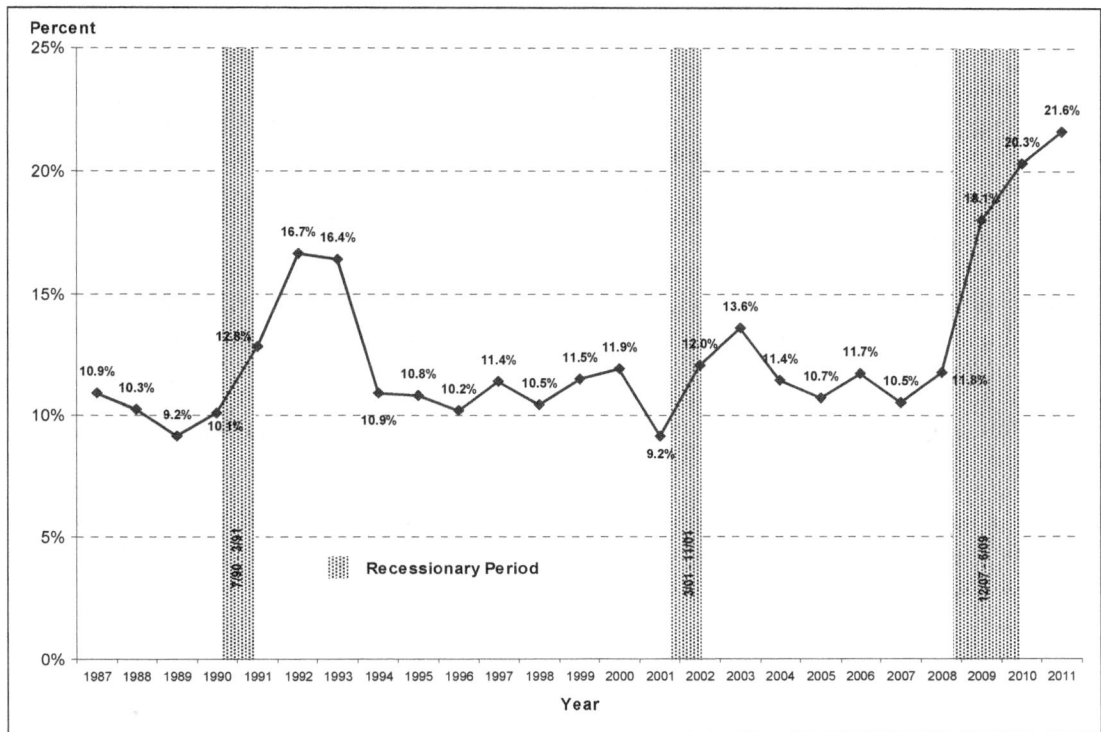

Source: CRS estimates from CPS/ASEC, 1988 to 2012.

Note: Based on UI benefits reported on the CPS/ASEC. Aggregate UI benefits reported on the survey under-represent actual dollars paid out as UI claims under state Unemployment Insurance trust funds. Among families considered poor before counting any UI benefits they received, UI dollars filling the "poverty gap" represent the aggregate amount of UI benefits going toward filling the shortfall in families' incomes from their respective poverty income thresholds.

Antipoverty Effect of UI Benefits Among Unemployed Individuals

Figure 12 compares poverty rates among *unemployed persons* by whether they received UI benefits during the year, or not. (The figure differs from **Figure 8**, shown previously, which was for *all persons in families* that received UI benefits). For those that received UI benefits, both their pre-UI poverty rates and post-UI poverty rates are shown. The figure shows, for example, that unemployed persons who received UI benefits had lower poverty rates, before counting any UI benefits they received, than unemployed persons who did not receive UI benefits.

Over the past recession, and the subsequent economic recovery, poverty rates among the unemployed have increased over their pre-recession levels, regardless of whether they received

UI benefits. The poverty rate among the unemployed not receiving UI benefits increased from a pre-recession low of 23.6% in 2006, to recent high of 30.1% in 2011 (top line). In contrast, among the unemployed who received UI benefits, their pre-UI poverty rate increased from 13.4% in 2007 to a recent high of 27.5% in 2010 (middle line). Over this period, UI recipients' pre-UI poverty status converged on that unemployed non-recipients—in 2007, UI recipients' pre-UI poverty rate was 10.4 percentage points below that of unemployed non-recipients (13.4% and 23.8%, respectively), and by 2010, just 2.2% below (27.5% and 29.7%, respectively). From 2010 to 2011, the gap has widened somewhat as the pre-UI poverty rate of UI recipients fell somewhat over the period, whereas that of non recipients continued to increase.

In most years, other than those immediately around recessionary periods, pre-UI poverty rates of persons who received UI benefits (middle line) ranged from 40% to 50% below those of their unemployed counterparts who did not receive UI benefits (top line). Immediately after recessionary periods the differences in poverty rates before UI receipt is calculated narrows. For example, in 1993, the pre-UI poverty rate of persons receiving UI benefits was 36% below that of persons not receiving UI; in 2003, 26% below; in 2009, 16% below, in 2010, just 7% below, and in 2011, 9% below.

UI benefits dramatically reduced the prevalence of poverty among the population who received them in the past recession and current recovery. In 2010, for example, over one quarter (27.5%) of unemployed people who received UI benefits would have been considered poor prior to counting the UI benefits they received (middle line); after counting UI benefits, their poverty rate was cut by well over half, to 12.5% (bottom line). In contrast, in the two previous recessions, UI benefits to the unemployed reduced their incidence of poverty from a pre-UI poverty rate of 18.9% to a post-UI poverty rate of 10.1% in 2003, and from 18.3% to 11.2% in 1993. Based on this, and the other evidence presented in this analysis, UI benefits in the most recent recession appeared to have played a significantly greater role in reducing poverty than in either of the two previous recessions.

Figure 12. Pre-Post UI Poverty Rates Among Unemployed Persons Who Received UI Benefits and Those Who Did Not, 1987-2011

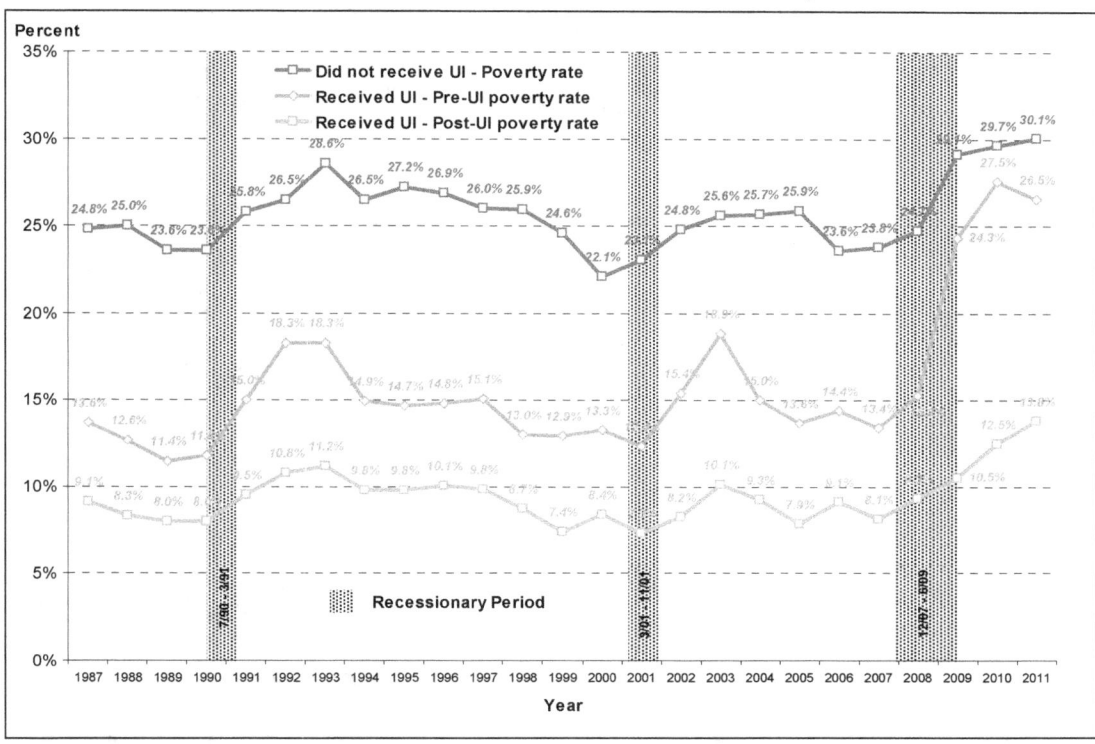

Source: CRS estimates from CPS/ASEC, 1988 to 2012.

Figure 13 depicts the share of unemployed persons who had no earnings during the year, by whether the individual received UI benefits during the year or not. The figure shows, for example, that in 2007, among unemployed during the year who received UI benefits, just over 1-in-20 persons (5.6%) had no earnings during the year. In comparison, among those unemployed who reported no UI receipt, over 1-in-5, 21.7%, had no earnings in 2007.

The share of unemployed UI recipients who had no earnings during the year increased during the most recent recession: from 1-in-10 (10.1%) in 2008; to over 1-in-5 (20.7%) in 2009; to over 1-in-4 (25.7%) in 2010; and just under that ratio (23.2%) in 2011. This trend corresponds to an increase in the median duration of unemployment among unemployed workers from 2007 to 2010, shown earlier in **Figure 2**. This pattern also is apparent in the administrative data shown earlier in **Figure 4** which showed an increased reliance among the unemployed on EB and EUC08, relative to regular UC benefits.

Figure 13. Share of Unemployed Persons Who Had No Earnings in the Year, by UI Receipt, 1987-2011

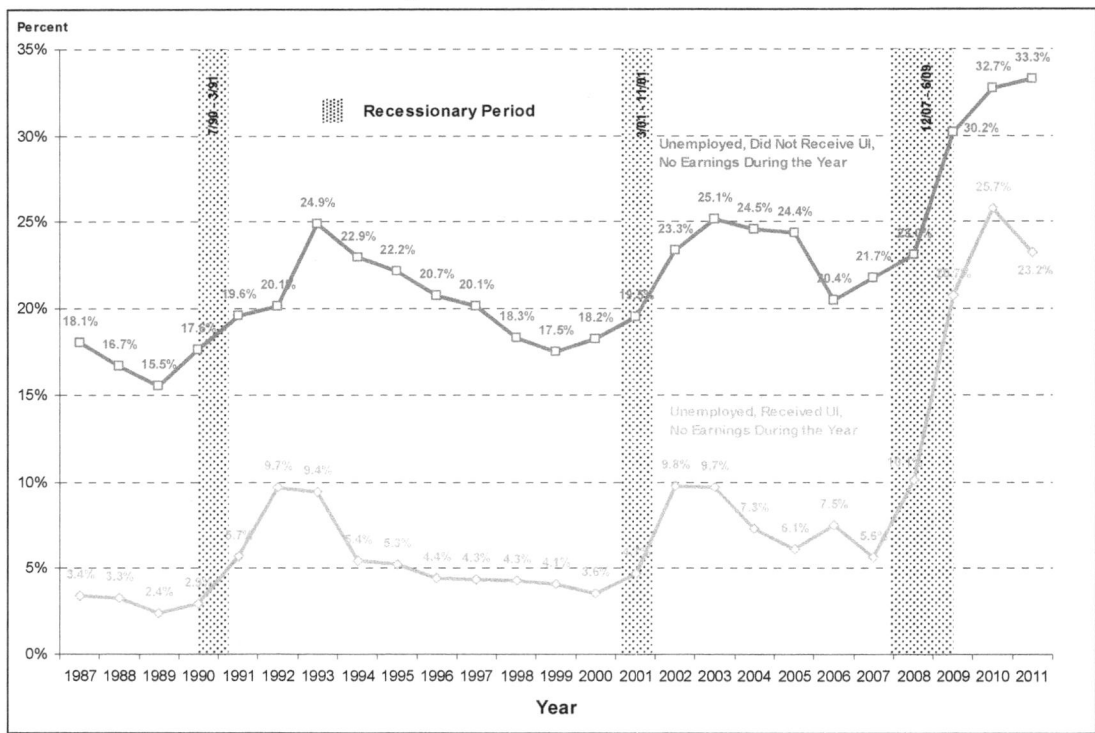

Source: CRS estimates CPS/ASEC, 1988 to 2012.

The increase in pre-UI poverty rates of unemployed UI recipients, the increased proportion of the unemployed receiving EB or EUC08 benefits, and the increased likelihood that unemployed UI recipients reported no earnings in the past year, suggest that the convergence of the pre-UI poverty rates (shown earlier in **Figure 12**) is a result of the increased duration of unemployment. In terms of the most recent recession and its aftermath, UI benefits (UC, EB, and EUC08) continue to appear to have a large poverty-reducing effect among unemployed workers who receive them. In particular, given the extended length of unemployment among jobless workers, the additional weeks of UI benefits beyond the regular UC program's approximately 26-week limit appear to have had an especially important effect in poverty reduction.

Summary

Our analysis shows that UI benefits appear to significantly reduce the incidence of poverty among the population who receives them. The UI benefits' poverty reduction effects appear to be especially important during and immediately after recessions. Our analysis also finds that there was a markedly higher impact on poverty in 2009 and 2010 than in the previous two recessionary periods. The estimated antipoverty effects of UI benefits in 2009 and 2010 were about twice that of two previous peak years of unemployment, in 1993 and 2003. This may be attributable to the temporary provisions of ARRA and the EUC08 program which increased both benefit levels and benefit duration.

- In 2011, well over one-quarter (26.5%) of unemployed people who received UI benefits would have been considered poor prior to counting the UI benefits they received; after counting UI benefits, their poverty rate was cut by almost half, to 13.8%.

- Because the U.S. poverty measure is based on the income of all co-resident related family members, UI receipt affects not only the poverty status of the person receiving the benefit, but the poverty status of all related family members, as well. In 2011, while an estimated 10.2 million people reported UI receipt during the year, an additional 15.8 million family members lived with the 10.2 million receiving the benefit. Consequently, UI receipt in 2011 affected the income status of some 26.0 million persons.

- The poverty rate for persons in families who received unemployment benefits in both 2009 and 2010 was approximately half of what it would have been without those unemployment benefits. In 2011, the poverty rate was 40% less than it would have been without these unemployment benefits.

- In 2011, UI benefits lifted an estimated 2.3 million people out of poverty, of which well over one quarter (26.8%; 620,000) were children living with a family member who received UI benefits.

Appendix A. Legislative Details of the Emergency Unemployment Compensation Program

On June 30, 2008, President George W. Bush signed the Supplemental Appropriations Act of 2008 (P.L. 110-252) into law. Title IV of this act created a new temporary unemployment insurance program, the Emergency Unemployment Compensation (EUC08) program. This was the eighth time Congress had created a federal temporary program that has extended unemployment compensation during an economic slowdown. The authorization for this program continues until the week ending on or before January 2, 2012.

The EUC08 program has been amended by P.L. 110-449, P.L. 111-5, P.L. 111-92, P.L. 111-118, P.L. 111-144, P.L. 111-157, P.L. 111-205, P.L. 111-312, P.L. 112-78, and P.L. 112-96. In July 2008, the program began with a flat 20 weeks of entitlement. In November 2008, P.L. 110-449 created an additional 13 week entitlement for workers in states with high unemployment for a total of 33 weeks of benefits available. This entitlement was expanded by an additional 20 weeks (up to 14 additional weeks in all states and 6 additional weeks in very high unemployment states) resulting in a potential of 53 weeks as required by P.L. 111-92 in November 2009. From November 2009 through February 2012, this temporary unemployment insurance program provided up to a total of 53 additional weeks of UI benefits (P.L. 111-118, P.L. 111-144, P.L. 111-157, P.L. 111-205, P.L. 111-312, and P.L. 112-78).[38] P.L. 112-96 created a complex set of alterations to the EUC08 program. From February 2012 through May 2012, EUC08 provided up to 63 additional weeks and then returned to providing up to 53 weeks in June 2012. Beginning in September 2012 through December 2012, the program provides up to 47 weeks of additional UI benefits.[39]

---

[38] The total unemployment rate is a three-month seasonally adjusted average of the state's monthly unemployment rate. For a detailed legislative history of the EUC08 program, see CRS Report RL34340, *Extending Unemployment Compensation Benefits During Recessions*, by Julie M. Whittaker and Katelin P. Isaacs.

[39] For details on the intricacies of the EUC08 program, see CRS Report R42444, *Emergency Unemployment Compensation (EUC08): Current Status of Benefits*, by Julie M. Whittaker and Katelin P. Isaacs

Appendix B. Trends in Labor Force Status and UI Receipt Over Time

This appendix presents an analysis of trends in labor force status and UI receipt, as reported in the U.S. Census Bureau's Annual Social and Economic Supplement to the Current Population Survey (CPS/ASEC). The analysis is based on labor force status in the year preceding the CPS/ASEC survey, based on survey respondents' accounts.

The appendix provides contextual reference of different measures of labor "underutilization," including monthly and annual monthly averages of unemployment compared to estimates for persons unemployed at *anytime during the year* (the definition of unemployed used in the report's CPS/ASEC analysis). It also examines and more expansive definitions of labor utilization, which in addition to unemployed (persons without a job who looked for work) includes involuntary part-time workers and discouraged workers (those who did not search for work believing suitable work is not available). The appendix examines UI receipt reported on the CPS/ASEC among persons of the above, and other, labor force statuses.

The CPS/ASEC collects information on over 50 sources of income, and up to 27 individual income values—UI benefits are among the many income sources and amounts captured by the survey, since 1988. CPS/ASEC survey respondents report their yearly income from each specific source. See **Appendix C** for a comparison of CPS/ASEC estimates of UI receipt and amounts with administrative benchmarks of UI claims and benefit amounts.

Unemployed Persons and Those with Limited Labor Force Attachment Relating to Economic Conditions Who Reported UI Receipt

Figure B-1 and **Figure B-2** show persons who reported UI benefit receipt and their labor force status in 2011, based on CRS analysis of the 2012 CPS/ASEC. The analysis primarily focuses on several groups of persons who are unemployed or who have *limited labor force attachment* over the year that may be associated with economic conditions. These groups are represented in **Figure B-1**. Among these groups are those who most likely might qualify for UI benefits. The groups (with the percentage of each group represented among persons who reported UI receipt in 2011) include

- "Unemployed" (70.3%): persons who reported having worked less than full year and looked for work during the year or were on layoff;

- "Involuntary part-time workers" (3.9%): persons who worked all year but reported having worked less than full time (35 or more hours per week) due to slack work or because they could only find part-time work;

- "Part-year discouraged workers" (2.6%): persons who worked only part year, but did not search for work because they believed no work was available.

In addition to the groups above, who were all in the labor force during the year by virtue of having had a job or looking for work, the analysis includes

- "Discouraged potential workers, outside the labor force" (2.5%): persons who were out of the labor force for the entire year and reported that they did not look for work because they believed no work was available.

The four groups delineated above represent those respondents on the CPS/ASEC who might most reasonably be expected to be among the population potentially qualified to receive UI benefits. They represent the majority of persons, 8.1 million (79.2%) of 10.2 million who reported receiving UI benefits in 2011, and constitute the major groups that appear to have had *limited work force/labor force attachment associated with economic conditions.*[40]

Other Labor Force Statuses of Persons Who Reported UI Receipt

Included among persons on the CPS/ASEC who report UI receipt, not all appear to have limited labor force attachment that might seem to be directly associated with economic conditions. These groups are depicted in **Figure B-2**. Reported receipt of UI among these cases is somewhat incongruent with their reported labor force status during the year. These groups that reported UI receipt include

- "Full-time, Full-Year Workers" (6.1%): persons who reported having worked full-time (35 or more hours per week), full-year (50 to 52 weeks) and did not look for work during the year;

- "Out of the labor force (OLF), full or part-year, for personal reasons" (12.6%): persons who were out of the labor force for part or the entire year (i.e., did not look for work during the period they were without work) and reported that the primary reason they were not working was because they were ill or disabled, taking care of home or family, going to school, or retired;

- "Voluntary part-time workers" (1.9%): persons who worked part time for the entire year, because they wanted part time work ;

- "Persons in the armed forces living off base" (negligible, 0.2%).

The somewhat anomalous report of UI among the above groups may be due to misreporting of UI benefit receipt itself, or imprecise reporting of their labor force attachment over the course of the year.[41] For example, in the latter case, a respondent may have been unemployed during part of the year, and later in the year enrolled in school, or decided to retire. Individuals who were enrolled in school may be eligible for unemployment benefits while attending Workforce Investment Act (WIA)-approved training programs.

---

[40] For more information on why alternative measures of unemployment statistics may be used, see U.S. Department of Labor, Bureau of Labor Statistics, *The Unemployment Rate and Beyond: Alternative Measures*, Issues in Labor Statistics, Summary 08-06, Washington, DC, June 2008, http://www.bls.gov/opub/ils/pdf/opbils67.pdf.

[41] Furthermore, there are several small programs that allow workers to receive unemployment benefits while working close to full-time hours. (See CRS Report R40689, *Compensated Work Sharing Arrangements (Short-Time Compensation) as an Alternative to Layoffs*, by Alison M. Shelton.) Under some state UI programs it is possible for the unemployed to be in training/educational pursuits as long as certain criteria are met.

Figure B-1. Persons Who Reported UI Benefit Receipt, by Labor Force Status: 2011

Unemployed, Underutilized, and Discouraged Workers Due to Economic Conditions (8.103 million persons)

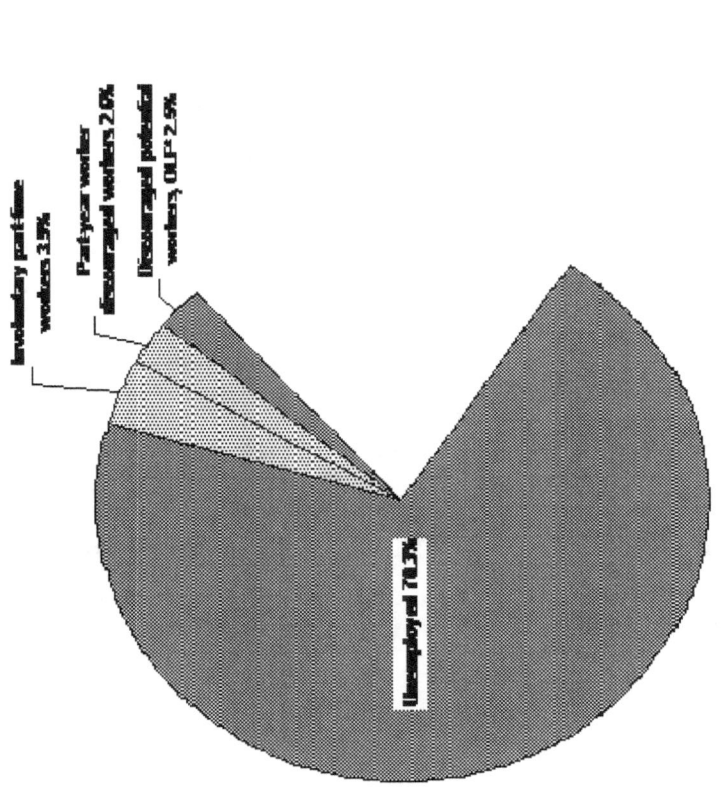

Figure B-2. Persons Who Reported UI Benefit Receipt, by Labor Force Status: 2011

Other Labor Force Statuses of Persons Reporting UI Receipt (2.123 million persons)

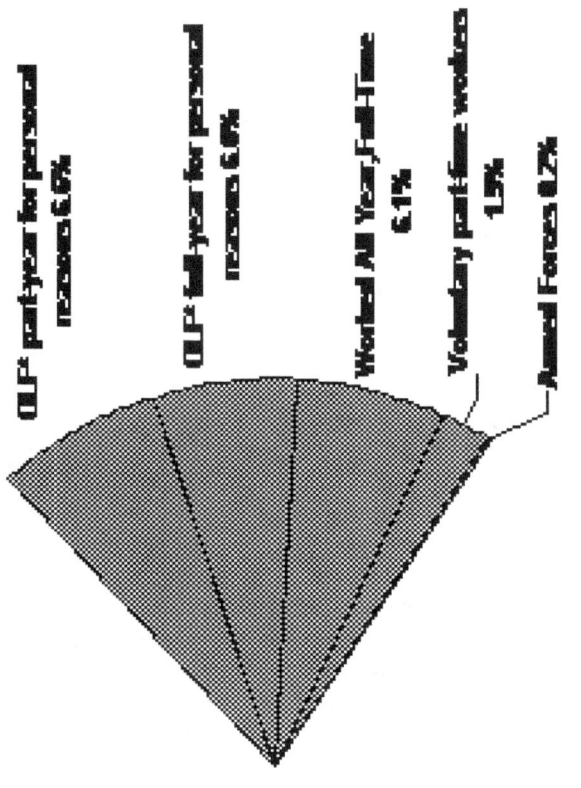

Source: Congressional Research Service (CRS) estimates from U.S. Census Bureau Current Population Survey Annual Social and Economic Supplement (CPS/ASEC), 2012.

Note: * Persons Outside the Labor Force (OLF).

Comparing the Share of Unemployed and Underutilized Workers at Any Time During the Year to Monthly and Annual Average Unemployment Statistics

Figure B-3 compares annual measures of unemployment and labor underutilization derived from CRS analysis of CPS/ASEC data with the monthly unemployment rate, and annual average monthly employment rate (as published by the BLS, based on the monthly CPS, presented at the beginning of this report in **Figure 1**).

It is important to note that CRS CPS/ASEC unemployment and labor underutilization rate estimates are based on survey respondents' accounting of their labor force status over an entire year. By this measure, a respondent would be considered unemployed if they were unemployed at any time during the year. The odds are greater that a person will be unemployed at any time during the year, than at a particular point in time during the year. Consequently, the CRS CPS/ASEC unemployment and labor underutilization measures are both higher than corresponding BLS monthly and annual average monthly measures. The BLS monthly unemployment rate peaked at 10.0% in October 2009; whereas, the annual average monthly rate for 2009 was 9.3%. In contrast, the CRS CPS/ASEC unemployment rate, measuring persons who were ever unemployed during the year as share of the labor force, was 13.0%—a full 3.3 percentage points above the annual average monthly rate. Similarly, the CRS CPS/ASEC underutilized worker rate was 19.5% in 2009; this compares with an annual average monthly rate for the BLS U-6 alternative unemployment measure of 16.3% for 2009.

Figure B-3. Share of Unemployed and Underutilized Workers at Any Time During the Year Compared with Monthly and Annual Average Unemployment

January 1987 to August 2012

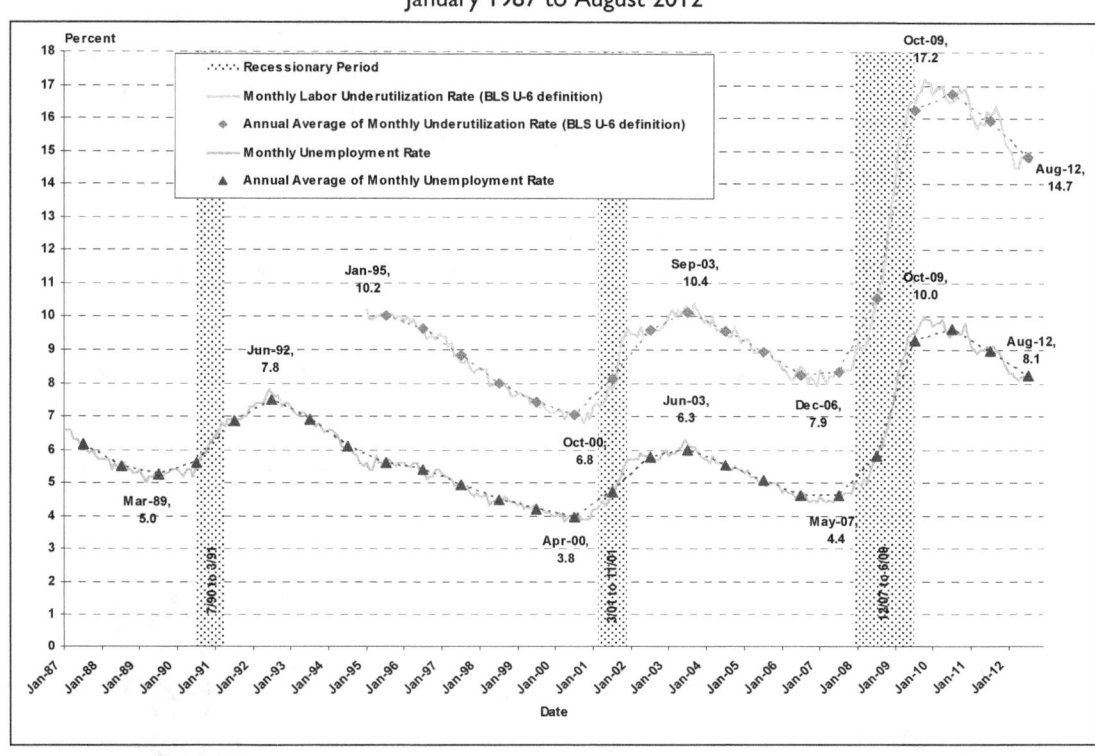

Source: Congressional Research Service (CRS) estimates from U.S. Census Bureau Current Population Survey Annual and Social and Economic Supplement (CPS/ASEC). 1988 to 2012; and U.S. Bureau of Labor Statistics (BLS) monthly unemployment rates, available at http://data.bls.gov/cgi-bin/surveymost?bls.

Notes:

Monthly and annual average of monthly unemployment rates from BLS monthly unemployment rates, available at http://data.bls.gov/cgi-bin/surveymost?bls.

CRS estimates from the CPS/ASEC of persons who where unemployed at any time during the year, as a share of labor force participants during the year plus "discouraged potential workers" outside the labor force.

CRS estimates from the CPS/ASEC of persons who where unemployed at any time during the year plus underutilized workers (part-year discouraged workers, involuntary part-time workers, and discouraged potential workers, outside the labor force) as a share of labor force participants during the year plus "discouraged potential workers" outside the labor force.

Trends in Unemployment and Alternate Measures of Labor Underutilization

Figure B-4 provides estimates of the number of persons whose job attachment may have been limited due to economic conditions. The labor force definition used here includes all civilians age 15 and older who held a job at any time during the year, or looked for work. In addition, it includes persons who were outside the labor force (OLF) for the entire year, who indicated that they did not search for work because they believed no work was available—a group categorized as "discouraged potential workers." This group is generally not included in the standard labor force definition. For brevity, the term labor force is used throughout the analysis, but it should be kept in mind that it includes "discouraged potential workers (DPW)."

As shown in **Figure B-4**, an estimated 23.8 million persons were unemployed at some time during 2011. Another 8.2 million were involuntary part-time workers, who desired more hours of work. An additional 1.7 million persons worked only part year, but did not search for work because they believed no work was available. Finally, another 1.9 million discouraged potential workers were outside the labor force for the entire year, indicating that they did not search for work because they believed no work was available. In total, in 2011, an estimated 35.6 million persons had limited or no labor force attachment during the year that may have been associated with economic conditions. This compares with an estimated 29.4 million such persons in 1993, and 24.2 million in 2003, which marked previous peaks of slack employment in the U.S. economy.

Figure B-4. Expanded Definitions of Unemployment and Labor Underutilization, 1987-2011

Numbers in millions

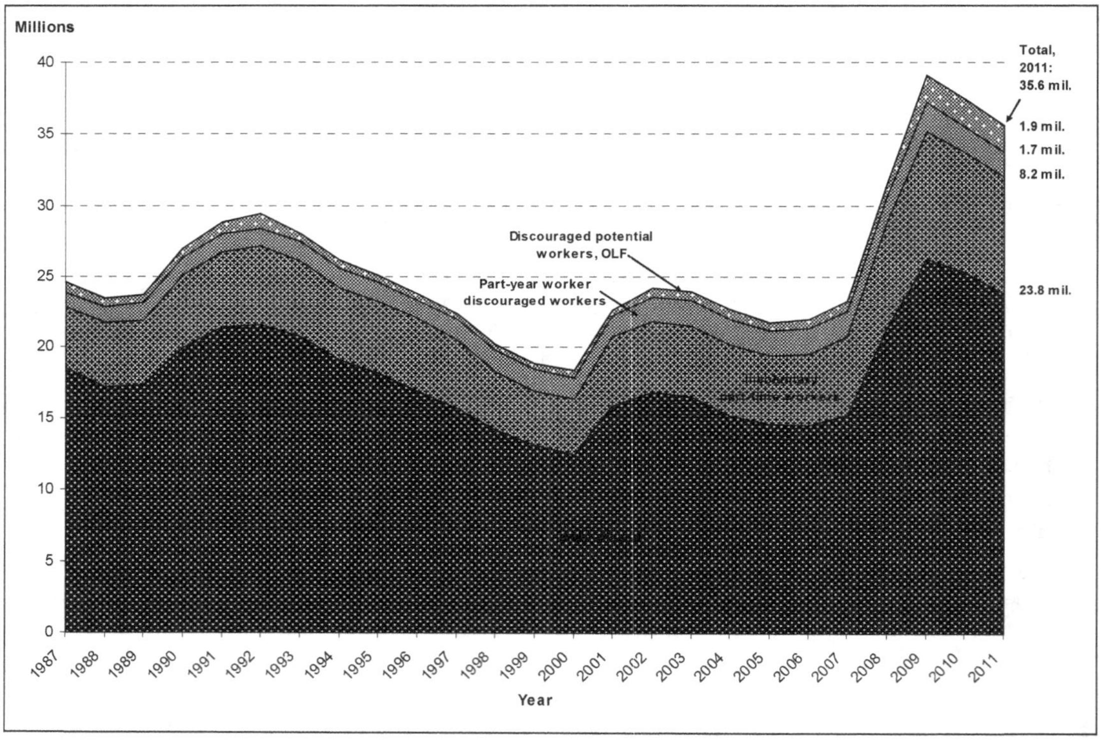

Source: Congressional Research Service (CRS) estimates from U.S. Census Bureau Current Population Survey Annual Social and Economic Supplement (CPS/ASEC), 1988 to 2012.

Figure B-5 shows that in 2009, an estimated 13.0% of the labor force was unemployed at some time during the year, which was similar to the earlier peak in 1991 and 1992 (12.9%).[42] The 1990-1991 recession contributed to the share of the labor force experiencing some period of

---

[42] The differences between the two peaks are not statistically significant.

unemployment rising from a pre-recession low of 10.9% in 1988, to a high of 12.9% in 1991 and 1992 (a 3 percentage point increase). In contrast, under the most recent recession, the share of the labor force experiencing some period of unemployment during the year rose from a pre-recession low of 8.0% in 2006, to 13.0% in 2009 (a 5.0 percentage point increase).

The figure shows that in 2011 over one-sixth of the labor force (18.0%) had limited labor force attachment for economic reasons, up from a pre-recession low of 12.1% in 2006 (a 6.1 percentage point increase). In addition to the unemployed, involuntary part-time workers accounted for 4.1% of the labor force, and part-year discouraged workers and discouraged potential workers each accounted for 0.9% of the labor force. The top line in **Figure B-5** presents the sum of each of these groups to create a total unemployment rate using this expanded definition of individuals who were unemployed and is the same as the top line in **Figure B-3**. While, much reduced from 2009 and 2010, the share of the labor force under this expanded definition of unemployed in 2011 continued to exceed (by 0.4 percentage points) the previous high of 17.6% in 1992.

Figure B-5. An Expanded Definition of Unemployed and Underutilized Workers, 1987-2011

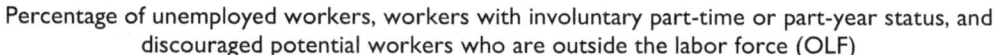

Percentage of unemployed workers, workers with involuntary part-time or part-year status, and discouraged potential workers who are outside the labor force (OLF)

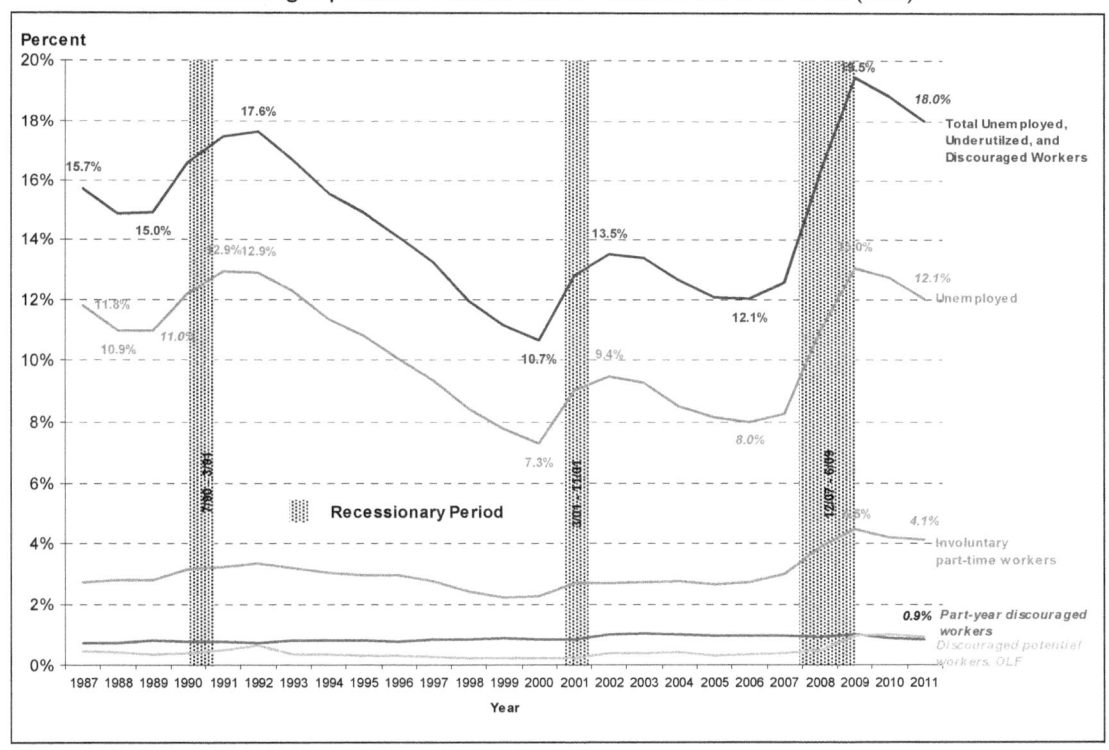

Source: Congressional Research Service (CRS) estimates from U.S. Census Bureau Current Population Survey Annual Social and Economic Supplement (CPS/ASEC), 1988 to 2012.

Unemployment Insurance Receipt Among Persons Who Were Unemployed or Who Had Limited or No Labor Force Attachment for Economic Reasons

Figure B-6 shows the share of persons who reported receiving UI benefits, by their labor force status during the year. The figure includes only persons who had limited or no labor force attachment during the year due to economic reasons or who met the CPS definition of unemployed. In 2011, these groups accounted for 8.1 million persons, or four-fifths (79.2%) of the 10.2 million who reported receiving UI benefits.

The figure shows that 30.2% of persons who were unemployed received UI benefits in 2011,[43] down from 2009 (36.1%), which was above the peak rates associated with previous recessions (34.4% in 1992 and 32.7% in 2002). The figure shows that the UI recipiency rate among discouraged potential workers who had been out of the labor force for the entire year remained high (13.5% in 2011, compared with highs of 12.5% in 1992, and 10.2% in 2003). However, as shown earlier in **Figure B-6**, this group accounts for only a small share of persons who had limited or no labor force attachment due to economic reasons. Among all persons with limited or no labor force attachment for economic reasons, 22.8% reported receipt of UI benefits in 2011, down from 2009 (27.4%)—the same share as the peak recipiency rate of 1992—and also below the 25.7% rate in 2002.

---

[43] Note, this estimate from the CPS/ASEC is considerably less than the 51% shown earlier in **Figure 4**, which is based on administrative data. For a discussion of CPS/ASEC estimates compared to administrative data benchmarks, see **Appendix C**.

Figure B-6. Unemployment Insurance Receipt Among Persons, by Selected Labor Force Status, 1987–2011

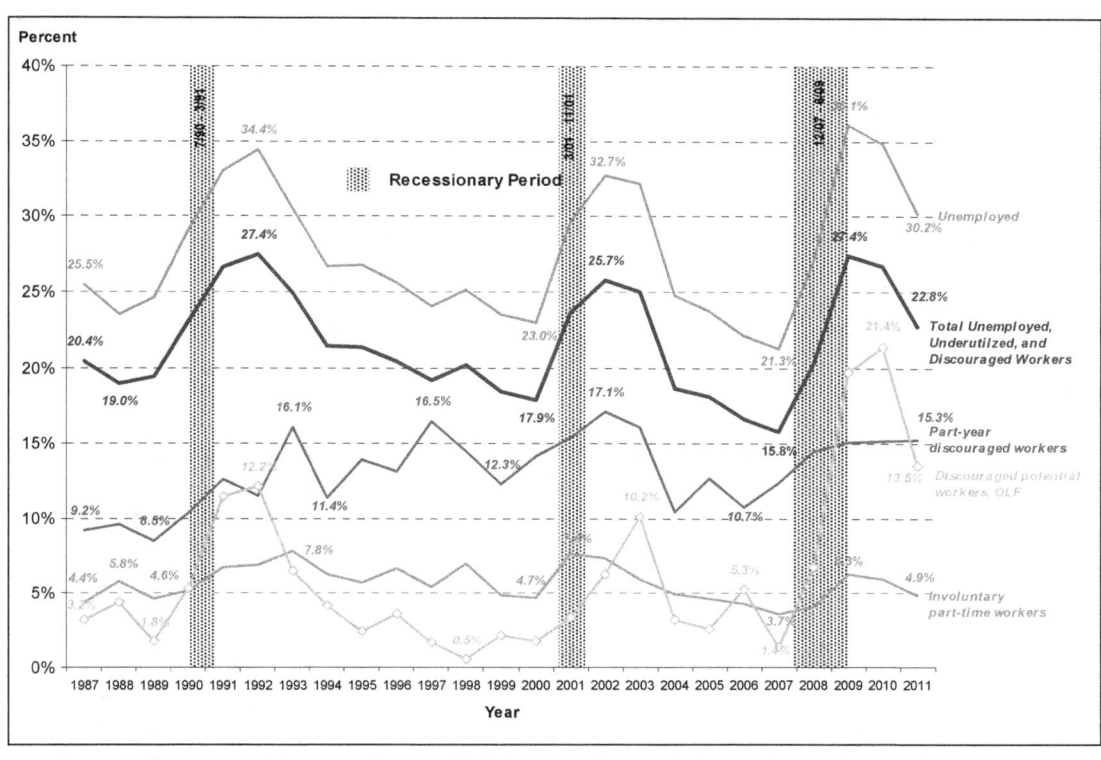

Source: Congressional Research Service (CRS) estimates from U.S. Census Bureau Current Population Survey Annual Social and Economic Supplement (CPS/ASEC), 1988 to 2012.

Appendix C. CPS/ASEC Estimates Versus Administrative Benchmarks

It is difficult to compare the monthly administrative UI data on the number of individuals receiving unemployment benefits to the one-time monthly survey CPS/ASEC data of those individuals who have reported receiving unemployment benefits in the past year. According to the U.S. Department of Labor (DOL) in 2011, approximately $103.7 billion in "unemployment benefits" were distributed to individuals. These benefits included UC, EB, and EUC08 as well as several smaller benefits such as the Disaster Unemployment Assistance and Trade Re-Adjustment Allowances. In comparison $68.5 billion in aggregate UI benefits were reported in the CPS/ASEC. Thus, in 2011, aggregate UI benefits reported on the CPS/ASEC accounted for about 66% of the administrative benchmark; approximately 34% of UI benefits in the aggregate were not reported/underreported—the largest level over the 25-year period examined (see the top line in **Figure C-1**).

The U.S. DOL does not calculate the number of individuals who received unemployment benefits at any point *during the year*, but rather it reports the number of individuals receiving benefits as a monthly statistic. Approximately 51% of the unemployed received unemployment benefits on average *in any given month* in 2011. Using the CPS/ASEC data, this analysis estimated that approximately 30% of the unemployed reported receiving a UI benefit at least for some point *during the year*.

There may be empirical reasons for the yearly ratio to be lower than the monthly ratio. One such reason is that generally those who receive unemployment benefit are likely to remain unemployed longer than those who do not receive such benefits. Thus, UI recipients may be appear in the monthly calculations for more months than non-UI recipients driving up the percentage of UI beneficiaries in the monthly calculations relative the annual calculations where both UI beneficiaries and non-beneficiaries are each counted one time. Given that the ratio of underreporting the total value of UI benefits is less than the ratio of underreporting UI benefit receipt this suggests that those who received lower values of aggregated UI benefits are more likely to not report benefit receipt.

Figure C-1 examines this pattern of under-reporting UI benefits by comparing estimates of aggregate UI benefits and number of recipients on the CPS/ASEC relative to DOL administrative benchmarks, from 1987 through 2011. The two lines depict the CPS/ASEC estimate as a percent of DOL administrative benchmarks based on UI spending and benefits data. CPS/ASEC estimates are for persons who reported having received any type of UI benefits at any time during the year. Estimates of the number of recipients from DOL UI administrative data are based on the total number of persons receiving UC benefits at the *beginning* of the year plus the total number of persons receiving *initial monthly UC benefits during the year* plus the number of persons receiving UC for former federal workers (UCFE), UC for former service members (UCX), Disaster Unemployment Assistance (DUA), Trade Readjustment Assistance (TRA), EB, EUC08 and the other temporary extended benefits at the *beginning of the year*.[44]

---

[44] Mathematically, this approach will result in counting the number of first week of regular UC beneficiaries twice and not counting any new entrants into the UCFE, UCX, and DUA program if the first benefit was paid after the first week of the new year.

Figure C-1 shows that aggregate benefits reported on the CPS/ASEC ranged from a low of 66% of the administrative benchmark in 2010 and 2011, to a high of 88% in 1995. As noted above, the CPS/ASEC does an apparently better job at capturing UI dollars, in the aggregate, than it does in the number persons receiving benefits. Over the period examined, the CPS/ASEC appears to capture roughly 59% of persons who receive UI benefits based on claims data with the ratio generally increasing during recessions and decreasing as the recovery takes hold. The ratio ranges from a low of 49% in 2004, 2006, and 2007, to a high of 73% in 1993. As noted above, the CPS/ASEC appears to do a better job in capturing aggregate UI dollars than it does in capturing UI recipients would suggest that persons who receive comparatively small UI benefits, and/or claim benefits for a comparatively short period of time, are less likely to report UI benefit receipt on the CPS/ASEC.

Figure C-1. UI Recipients and Aggregate UI Dollars CPS/ASEC Estimates as a Percent of Administrative Benchmarks, 1987-2011

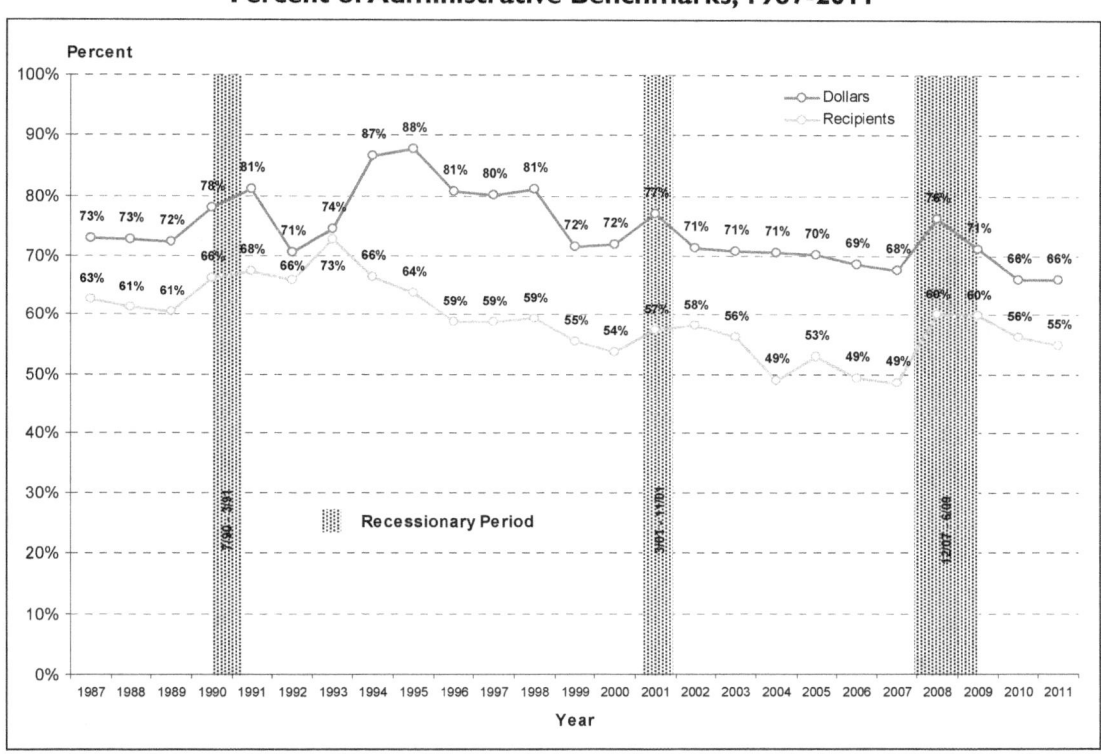

Source: Congressional Research Service (CRS) estimates from U.S. Census Bureau Current Population Survey Annual Social and Economic Supplement (CPS/ASEC), 1988 to 2012; and DOL Unemployment Insurance Reporting System.

Notes: Recipient estimates are based on reported receipt of UI on the CPS/ASEC and DOL UI claims data. CPS/ASEC estimates are for persons who reported having received any type of UI benefits at any time during the year. Estimates of the number of recipients from DOL UI administrative data are based on the total number of persons receiving UC benefits at the *beginning* of the year plus the total number of persons receiving *initial monthly UC benefits during the year* plus the number of persons receiving DUA, UC for federal workers, UC for ex-military service members, trade readjustment assistance, EB, EUC08, and the other temporary federal extended benefits at the *beginning of the year.*

Author Contact Information

Thomas Gabe
Specialist in Social Policy
tgabe@crs.loc.gov, 7-7357

Julie M. Whittaker
Specialist in Income Security
jwhittaker@crs.loc.gov, 7-2587